Somewhere in the Gray

by

Joi Renee

ISBN: [979-8-9988429-0-0]

Cover design by Joi Renee

Printed in the United States of America

First Edition

For more information, visit: instagram.com/JoiReneeTheWriter

In loving memory of

La'Kaylia "Kay" Kea

"Live—boldly and with purpose—

in honor of the ones we've loved and lost,

who no longer have the chance to."

— Joi Renee

Table of Contents

INTRODUCTION

Why I'm Writing This Book:

Writing has always been my safe space. It's the one place where I don't have to hear the voice of myself or anyone else—I can just be. When I write, I (almost) never overthink or feel fearful. The parts of me that hold back in real life don't tend to exist when I'm putting words on a page. It's as if I step into a world where I am fully, unapologetically myself—no hesitation, no second-guessing, no waiting.

But for as long as I've loved writing, I've always had this lingering desire to write a book—and somehow, I kept putting it off. The when was always some distant moment in the future, some undefined time when I would finally feel ready. And yet, what I've come to realize is this:

I am ready now because now is all I have.

For a long time, I lived too much in the future, worrying about what was next, waiting for the right time, waiting to feel certain, waiting to be someone who no longer hesitated. Other times, I lived too much in the past, overanalyzing what was, replaying moments, and convincing myself that history would dictate my future. But the truth is, yesterday and tomorrow don't exist. The only thing that exists is right now.

And right now? I'm writing this book.

I also believe that our lives, our experiences, and our lessons are not just for us. I have been deeply moved, inspired, and changed by the words of others—whether in books, music, films, podcasts, or conversations. And if something I write can make even one person feel seen, understood, or less alone—then this book has already done what it was meant to do.

But even if the only life this book changes is my own, that is still more than enough for me.

What This Book Is (And What It Isn't):

This book is not a self-help book.

It's not a guide, a set of instructions, or a list of rules for how to live your life. It's not me telling you what's right or wrong. It's not me claiming to have all the answers. This book is a conversation. It's me showing up, being transparent, and giving you a front-row seat to my thoughts, my experiences, and my lessons. It's me reflecting in real-time, trying to make sense of the gray areas, and inviting you to do the same. It's a book about what I've learned so far. It's a book about how I see things now. It's a book about how I process, how I question, and how I grow. It's not a book just about writer-hood, grief, love, or friendship. It's a book about the gray areas within all of those parts of my life.

Each chapter will explore a specific space where I found myself caught between clarity and confusion, knowing and doubting, becoming and breaking. Because that's where most of life happens—in the tension between extremes. And because of that, some things I write here might change for me over time. Growth isn't about standing still in one perspective forever—it's about evolving, shifting, and learning as you go. That's why I say: take what resonates, leave what doesn't. There is no one-size-fits-all approach to life, and I'm not here to pretend there is. But what I do know is this: I am not alone in how I see the world, and neither are you.

So if you've ever felt like life doesn't fit neatly into black and white... If you've ever wrestled with the in-between... If you've ever wished someone else could just get it—this book is for you.

But even if that's not you— Even if you see the world through a more black-and-white lens, this book is still for you.

Because life is about perspective. And it says something about your character when you're willing to explore ones that aren't your own.

No, I'm not here to change your mind. But I am here to offer you another lens. One that might not shift your beliefs, but could stretch your understanding."

The Power of the Gray:

One of my favorite sayings is "Two things can be true at once." Because they can. Life is not either/or. It is both/and. Growth isn't linear. Healing isn't clean. Love isn't simple. Everything is layered. Everything is complex. And instead of fearing that complexity, what if we embraced it?

For so long, I wanted clear answers, black-and-white clarity, and definitive truths. But what I've come to learn is that the most beautiful, transformative, and meaningful moments in life happen in the gray.

The gray is where we learn. The gray is where we evolve. The gray is where we sit with our questions, our uncertainties, and our contradictions—and realize that we are still whole, even in the unknown.

And self-awareness? That's the key. That's how you navigate the gray. You may not be able to control everything in life, but you can control how you show up in it. The more you know yourself, the more you own your emotions, your choices, and your patterns—the more power you have. Because at the end of the day, the only thing you ever truly have control over is you.

So instead of fearing the gray, let's explore it. Let's sit in it. Let's make peace with the uncertainty and find meaning within it.

How This Book Works

Each chapter in this book is centered around a specific gray area of my life.

You'll notice that every title begins with The Gray Area of... followed by a theme—certainty, identity, grief, change, etc.

Within each of those themes, I'll walk you through a personal experience—something I lived through, questioned or wrestled with in real-time. You'll see the specific situations that brought that gray area to life and the thoughts, feelings, and decisions I had to work through in the moment.

Every chapter is structured in two parts:

1. The Unpacking – The raw experience. The inner dialogue. The moment I opened the drawer, pulled everything out and sat with the mess. The feelings that hadn't been sorted yet. The confusion that hadn't been named. The story before I had a clear understanding of what it all meant.

2. The Understanding – The insight I gained. The layered clarity I arrived at—not just about what happened, but about who I was inside of it. Understanding is not about black-and-white answers; it's about seeing the whole picture. The black, the white, and the gray. I don't just see it clearly—I see it fully. With all its nuance, contradiction, and complexity.

Some chapters will be long. Some will be short. All of them will be as long as they need to be. Because some lessons unfold slowly. Others crash in all at once.

More than anything, I want this book to feel like we're sitting together, having a deep conversation—like you're stepping into my world for a little while, and then stepping back into your own with a new perspective, a new question to ask yourself, or a new truth to hold.

And when you finish reading, I hope you feel like I was there with you. Because that's what I want most—for this book to feel like a companion to your own journey, just as much as it is a reflection of mine.

So here we are. Not in the past. Not in the future. But right here.

Somewhere in the Gray.

Chapter 1: The Gray Area of Certainty

From Control to Consciousness

The Unpacking

At 21, I was technically in a good place. I was finishing my junior year of college, surrounded by friends who were also stepping into this milestone year of turning 21. It was fun and exciting, and on the surface, everything seemed like it was falling into place. I was on track to earn my degree, celebrating the grind finally paying off, and feeling the thrill of adulthood becoming real. But underneath that surface-level joy, there was a strange cloudiness I didn't know how to name.

I had learned so much about myself in those college years, but I hadn't had the time—or maybe the courage—to sit down and sort through any of it. It felt like I was standing in front of a scattered puzzle. All the pieces were laid out, but none of them were connected. I couldn't see the bigger picture yet, and I didn't even know what I hoped it would look like. I was excited, but I was anxious. I was doing well, but I felt lost. I was surrounded by people, but a deep loneliness was starting to creep in. Spiritually, I was disconnected—still believing in God, but without a real relationship to hold on to. He was more of a concept than a companion. I didn't know what I was missing, so I didn't know to look for more. Then this relationship entered my life. And everything shifted.

What it was... wasn't easily defined. There was no clean label. But it quickly became one of the most important connections I've ever experienced. And looking back, I now know we were both trying to survive something. I had things I needed at that moment—so did he—and somehow, we became those things for each other. Two people with empty cups, doing the impossible: pouring into each other anyway. I still don't fully understand how it worked. But it did.

We talked every single day. Text threads, phone calls, hours-long parked car conversations that sometimes ended with us falling asleep and waking up in the same space just to talk more. Overnight visits that were filled with presence more than anything else. Even the silly moments, like him putting me on speaker in the passenger seat, buckling the phone in the seatbelt, and telling me I was "riding with him" to get food. It was always like that. Always "with," even when we weren't physically together.

I had never spent so much time with someone—not just in a romantic sense, but period. Even with my closest friends, our conversations would ebb and flow, our presence would be more event-based. But this? This was day-to-day, soul-to-soul, minute-to-minute type connection. And it became my lifeline.

I remember my final semester of college. I had to go back for one extra term in the winter of 2019, and I was living alone in a single dorm room. My days were routine and quiet, but he was always there. I'd go to class, text him in between, go to dinner alone, and sit in a booth long after I was done eating just to talk to him about our days, our fears, our ideas, our trauma, our wins, our losses—everything. There was no version of myself I couldn't be in that space. It was the safest place I had ever known.

And because of how rare and deep the connection was, I started to question it. How do you even categorize something like that? Is it romantic? Is it platonic? Even those labels didn't feel wide enough to hold what it was. And as confusing as that sounds, it didn't feel confusing in the beginning when I was in it. It felt divine. It felt like God had handcrafted someone specifically to understand me—someone who could meet me where I was without me having to explain myself. Someone who could name my emotions before I did. Someone who introduced me to myself.

It was the kind of connection that made me believe—for the first time ever—that maybe God didn't just create me for me, but also with someone else in mind. That kind of sacredness will shake you. But I was young. I was unhealed in ways I didn't know yet. I was used to emotional abandonment and unmet expectations. And the more I saw how deeply I could be transformed by this connection, the more afraid I became of losing it. So I started expecting the worst. And because I couldn't find anything "wrong enough" I started telling myself it was too good to be true. I convinced myself that at some point, it would turn into what everything else had been—and I didn't want to wait around for that. So I sabotaged it. But not loudly. Not all at once.

First, I let the fear settle in. Then I started searching for something to justify leaving. Something I could hold up to myself and say, "This is why it had to end." Eventually, I found something—a new relationship, one that came with a commitment I could point to. Something definitive. Something I could name. It gave me a reason to walk away. And I did. And while that new relationship was real, and I genuinely cared, it made it easy to disconnect from something I was too afraid to face.

Because here's the truth: that first relationship did everything opposite of what my past traumas had done to me. And because it didn't feel familiar, I waited for it to become traumatic. I couldn't trust what felt safe because it wasn't what I had known. And in that fear, I did the very thing I was afraid would happen to me: I abandoned something that meant everything to me.

It wasn't about the label. It was about needing something black and white to hold onto—something clear enough to protect me from the uncertainty. I thought if I defined it, I could control it. But I never gave it a chance to become what it was meant to be. I never asked for clarity. I didn't even give him the opportunity to let me down—because I didn't want to feel the sting of disappointment from someone who meant that much. So instead, I left first. I chose control over connection.

The full weight of what I did didn't hit me until later. Until I lost myself. Until I no longer had him to lead me back to me. And because I had relied on his direction, I didn't know how to lead myself back on my own. I spiraled. I slipped into depression—stacked on top of postpartum depression when I later had my son—and I realized how deeply I had hurt someone who never tried to hurt me.

And even now, I give myself grace. I was young. I was scared. I didn't know what I didn't know. But none of that erases the pain I caused. I forgive myself. But the pain still lingers. Because, as I said, two things can be true.

I didn't understand that this situation—this relationship—didn't need to be defined to be honored. I thought it had to be yes or no. Black or white. Stop or go. But that way of thinking didn't fit this.

And here's the part I can admit now, I wasn't even in a space to give definitive, black-and-white answers. The clarity I was demanding from him? I couldn't have offered it myself. It wasn't about being ready for a commitment or a label—it was about trying to regain control in a space that felt too unpredictable, too vulnerable, too unguarded. The uncertainty terrified me. And when you're terrified, control starts to look like protection—even if it's not.

That's why this was the experience that birthed my understanding of the gray. Because it made me realize that I don't think clearly in black and white. I don't exist fully in just black or white. And while I'm capable of drawing a line when I need to, I don't get there without navigating my way through the gray first. It's not my weakness—it's just the truth of how I experience life. And now, I honor that.

There's one piece I can't leave out—because it was the moment that truly forced me to explore the gray. For all the reflection I've done, for all the grace I've learned to extend, here's something I have to admit: when I became fully aware of the impact my actions had on him, I was crushed.

I'm not someone who avoids accountability. In fact, I often face it head-on. In this situation, that meant sitting with the hard truth that while I don't regret the personal growth and blessings that came after removing myself from the situation—I do regret the mess I left behind. The heartbreak. The confusion. The pain I caused him.

And that's where the gray area lives. Because I wasn't someone who didn't love him. I wasn't careless. I wasn't cold. I didn't make a habit of ignoring his needs or withholding compassion. I made one bad judgment call—one act of self-protection disguised as forward movement—that caused very real harm.

And the way it played out? It looked selfish. It looked like I discarded him. Like I didn't care. Like the relationship meant nothing to me. And while that's not how it felt on the inside, I don't get to control how it landed. I don't get to rewrite the impact.

I had the right to leave. But the way I handled it? That matters. Especially when someone has poured so much into you, shown up for you, and created space for your healing. The door to leave may always be there, but how you walk through it—that's where your character lives.

People love to say, "If they loved you, they wouldn't have hurt you." The statements that sound neat and clean and irrefutable. But I've learned that those sayings don't always resonate with me. And I want to be really clear here—because I know how easily this part can be misunderstood.

This is not to encourage you to excuse or re-evaluate people who've harmed you. Some people are just selfish. Some people do not love you. Some people do hurt you intentionally—and they do so without care, without regard, without any hesitation. And when that's the case, the pain is not just real—it's revealing.

But this is why I say things aren't always black and white. Because sometimes, the pain someone causes you has nothing to do with how they feel about you—and everything to do with how they feel about themselves.

In my case, that's what it was. I didn't hurt him because I didn't love him. I didn't hurt him because I didn't care. I made a fear-driven decision that caused someone pain. And while I stand by my right to remove myself from a dynamic that felt emotionally overwhelming, I do not excuse the way I handled it.

Even when harm is unintentional, it still leaves a mark. And trauma may be the reason I acted the way I did—but it is not an excuse. My trauma doesn't cancel out the pain I caused. And that's the thing about the gray: I can understand why I did what I did, offer myself grace, and still fully acknowledge the weight of what it did to him.

And just as I have the right to walk away from a situation for my own safety, he has every right to remove me from his life in response to that harm. Whether or not he forgives me, whether or not he understands why I did it, whether or not he believes I meant it– closure isn't owed. Access isn't guaranteed. And even when things are complex—even when there's love, reason, and nuance involved—that doesn't mean reconciliation has to happen. That's the part we don't talk about enough. Even in the gray, people are allowed to set boundaries. Even in the gray, people are allowed to let go.

The Understanding

I used to think control would bring me peace. That if I could just name what something was—put it in a box, give it a label, wrap it up neatly—that certainty would protect me from confusion, disappointment, or pain. But what I've come to realize is that demanding clarity isn't always about being ready for an answer. Sometimes, it's just a method of regaining control because the gray feels too terrifying to sit with.

That was me. I wasn't in a space to provide black-and-white answers, but I wanted them anyway. Not because I was ready to offer them back, but because I thought they would calm the anxiety. That they'd help me feel safer. I thought if I could define the connection, I could control the outcome. But control doesn't equal peace. And clarity that's forced isn't real clarity—it's fear disguised as structure.

These days, I still have to check in with myself. I still have moments where the desire for control creeps in. But I remind myself: I'm not who I used to be. I love myself now. I respect myself. My cup is full—and not because someone else poured into it, but because I did. That's what makes the difference. Because when your peace comes from within, you're not as shaken by what's undefined.

Now, when something isn't clearly labeled or doesn't make perfect sense, I can pause. I can ask myself questions. I can examine the moving parts. I can look at the gray and wonder: What is this here to teach me? What's being revealed? What's still unfolding? And I can do that without abandoning myself in the process. Because today, I am a safe space for myself. Back then, I wasn't.

This experience taught me so much about love—but more importantly, it taught me about myself in love. I learned that just because you're good at giving love doesn't mean you're good at receiving it. I learned what unconditional love actually means. Not love without boundaries, but love that continues to exist in its purest form—even when the relationship changes. Even when it ends. And I now see how powerful it is to both offer and receive that kind of love.

I navigate relationships differently now. I check myself often. I ask: Am I being led by love? Or am I moving under the influence of fear and past trauma? Because when I lead with love—especially love for myself—I'm never disappointed. Even when something doesn't work out the way I hoped, I can still stand tall in how I showed up.

But when I move from fear? When I react instead of reflect? That's when I know I'm not acting from my true self. That's when I know I'm living in response to what hurt me, instead of from the truth of who I am—and who God created me to be.

And while I'm not perfect (and don't aim to be), my self-awareness has become my anchor. I know how to call myself out.

I know how to course-correct. And that's not something I could say back then.

This particular experience introduced me to the gray better than any other. Because this is when I met myself—truly. This wasn't the first self-defining moment of my life, but it was the deepest one. And while other moments in my past may have taken place in the gray, this was the one that brought me into the consciousness of it. This was the lens-shifting moment. And once I had that lens, I could go back and reprocess other moments—see where I'd rushed, where I'd judged too quickly, where I'd avoided complexity—and offer grace to both myself and others.

What I hope you take from this chapter is that the gray area is inevitable. Whether you acknowledge it or not, it's still there—just like a stop sign you might choose to run. You can pretend it's not real, but there may still be consequences for moving past it too fast. Instead, acknowledge it. Stop. Sit in it. Learn how to become a safe space for yourself so that the gray doesn't feel so threatening.

And no, I'm not trying to convince anyone that clarity doesn't matter. It does. But everything in life is not just one thing or the other. Remember, there's beauty in both/and.

If you're in a place right now where you're trying to force clarity—where you're anxious for answers—I'd invite you to slow down and check in with yourself. Ask yourself: Why do I feel like I need this answer right now? What's making me so uncomfortable with not knowing? Stay rooted in your values. Stay clear on your desires. But also recognize that sometimes, patience reveals more than pressure ever could.

This chapter is where I offer you the lens I now use for everything. These are the glasses I hope you wear while reading the rest of this book. Because from here on out, we'll walk through identity, grief, discouragement, detachment, and more—but always through the lens of the gray.

This chapter isn't just a story. It's the foundation. And if you're willing to sit with the discomfort of not always knowing for sure, you might just discover parts of yourself you didn't know were waiting to be seen.

Chapter 2: The Gray Area of Identity

Called by God, Unqualified by Society (or maybe just myself)

The Unpacking

The decision to place this chapter at the beginning of the book was intentional—because this chapter, and this book as a whole, is part of the proof I once thought I needed. Proof that I'm a writer. For a long time, I struggled to own that identity without an extensive portfolio, an outstanding resume, or external validation. That's why I call this chapter Called by God, Unqualified by Society—because that's exactly how it felt. Deep down, in my mind, my heart, my body, and my spirit, I knew I was created to write. But without the accolades, the publishing deals, the recognition, or the so-called "success," I didn't feel like I had the right to claim it. I was holding onto a truth God spoke over me while trying to reconcile it with a world that hadn't yet acknowledged it. That tension is where this chapter begins.

I had to ask myself: When did I actually start saying it out loud? When did I first begin to claim what I knew deep down was true?

The thing is—I never used to tell people I was a writer. That's what makes this question interesting because this answer helps me realize how long I carried the knowing without ever saying it out loud.

I started college at the University of Michigan in 2015. I went in already knowing I wanted to write. Back then, I thought I wanted to major in journalism. That dream stemmed from early high school when I was obsessed with the idea of one day having my own magazine. So I chose communications as my major, thinking it would align with that. But I didn't thrive in those classes like I expected. I didn't dominate them. I didn't feel lit up or energized. Some I enjoyed—like Mass Media Communications—but there was still this lingering feeling that something was... off. I wasn't ready to pivot just yet, but my antennas were up. I started to wonder: Am I wrong about what I want to do? Am I not meant to write? I kept going, but quietly, I was questioning everything.

Around that same time, I was struggling in Spanish, so I got a tutor—this girl who was super sweet and easy to talk to. While we studied, we also got to know each other, and I told her about my interest in magazines. She mentioned her friend was the president of a student org called Boundless—an online student magazine that highlighted women of color on campus. I immediately lit up. It felt like the perfect blend of purpose and possibility.

At that point, I didn't have many deep friendships in college yet. My friendships were still surfacy that first year. I'd grown up with the same group of friends back home, so starting fresh wasn't easy for me. I saw Boundless not just as a chance to write, but also as a way to connect with other Black women and maybe finally find my people.

I applied, got in, and started with the org my sophomore year as secretary and even became the president by the end of my junior year. I really did enjoy it—the work, the community, the creativity. But I still wasn't sure if having a magazine was my ultimate dream. I knew I loved writing. That was solid. But something still felt incomplete.

Then, one day I was making a slideshow for a mass meeting we were hosting—introducing the board, listing everyone's name, photo, major, all that. One of the girls' majors was Screen Arts and Cultures—and something about that title just grabbed me. I'd never even heard of it.

I looked it up on the university website, which listed all the possible careers that aligned with the major. It ranged from filmmaker to media lawyer, and everything in between. But what grabbed me the most was the idea of screenwriting. I felt this obsessive pull that I couldn't ignore.

I realized what journalism had been missing for me: imagination. With journalism, I was only writing about reality. And while I respected that, it felt... hobbyish. Like something I could do, but not something that made my spirit come alive. It didn't give me the freedom to expand or dramatize or let my mind go where it naturally wanted to go. I have a huge imagination—I just didn't know how valuable that was yet. I didn't label it as anything special back then. I thought that's just how everybody thought.

I've always daydreamed. I can zone out and create an entire movie scene in my head from the smallest real-life moment. I've always imagined experiences like that—planning something with a friend and picturing the future memory of it like a cinematic moment. It's how I move through the world. I see life in stories.

So when I discovered screenwriting, it was like the missing piece. I love writing stories grounded in reality—I don't typically do sci-fi or fantasy—but I want to take those real themes and amplify them. I want to dramatize life in a way that makes people feel. I live for tearjerkers. I want to write something that makes people cry, that makes them laugh, and that makes them pause and feel like they're in it. I want my writing to be immersive.

I switched my major to Screen Arts and Cultures. That was the first real step. But even then, I wasn't writing full-length scripts yet, so I wasn't telling anyone how much I dreamed of doing so.

During sophomore year, over Christmas break, I bought myself a Canon Rebel T6i camera off Amazon. It came with the full package—tripod, memory cards, lenses, all of it. My niece's mom had once told me I had a great eye, and photography had always been a hobby of mine. I even had a photography internship in high school.

So I started doing photography as a side hustle. Because of that, most people assumed that's what I was in school studying. They thought my major was photography because I never talked about screenwriting. And I didn't correct them.

It's not that I was ashamed—but I wasn't comfortable saying it out loud. How could I tell people I'm a screenwriter if I'm not putting anything out there? I didn't have a portfolio. I didn't have writing samples that I had the courage to share. I didn't have proof. It didn't make sense to me to claim it.

But the wild part is—I was that in my mind. It meant everything to me. That's where the whole dreamer vs. doer thing comes in. I wasn't fully doing it yet, but I was it in my head. I was dreaming it so hard. It meant so much that I had to protect it. So I let people believe photography was the dream—even though it wasn't.

And there were so many times I tried to write something that I would feel confident in sharing and stopped myself. Years ago, I started a note in my phone called "Script Ideas." That was supposed to be the beginning. But I let those ideas sit for years. I still have that note. And one of those ideas turned into the first full-length feature script I ever wrote. It had been in me for a long time. I just didn't know how to begin.

Even during the pandemic, when the world shut down and we were all stuck inside—I told myself I'd finally write. I had the time. I made a whole declaration: By the end of this summer, I'm going to write a Black romance movie. Never wrote it. I don't even know why I didn't. I can't point to a specific thought that stopped me. It's just... I didn't.

Looking back, I think I was scared. Scared that if I gave it my all and it still went nowhere, I'd have nothing left. But if I kept dreaming about it, at least I still had hope. The dream stayed alive.

But it was always just out of reach. And that's not worth it. Because then the dream isn't real—it's an illusion. And I don't want this part of me to be an illusion. I believe God put this fire in me. I feel made for this. There's nothing I want more than to write.

What finally pushed me over the edge was a significant life event that made me feel like I had hit rock bottom. I won't go into the details, but I'll say this: all I had left was me. And to hold onto me, I had to remember who I was. And who I was... was a writer. I had to become the version of me I believed in. The one I daydreamed about. The me that God intended. And that version of me writes.

So I started. I had this moment when I saw an organization for Black female screenwriters, but it was only for high school or college students. I DMed them and asked if they knew of anything for people in their 20s, and they directed me to Hillman Grad—Lena Waithe's Foundation. The applications for their mentorship program were open. I told myself, even if nothing comes of this, I'm going to apply. Because this will be the year I finally pursue it.

I wanted to write about young Black people and healing. That was the theme. That was the heartbeat. So I wrote the pilot for a TV series called Healing. It's not my best work. It's not even one of my favorites. But I will always love it because of what it represents. It marks the moment I became a writer out loud—not just in my head.

I wrote the first scenes lying in bed, typing on Google Docs from my phone. This was 2022, three years post-grad, and I had to dig into my memory from college classes just to remember formatting. I didn't go into the screenwriting sub-major, so I'd never actually written a full-length script in school. I was figuring it out as I went.

When my son was with his dad and I had some alone time, I would walk to the coffee shop behind my apartment, bring my laptop, and just... write. That coffee shop saved me. It's still one of my favorite seasons of life. I had my favorite spot to sit—my little unassigned, assigned seat. I was being intentional. I was showing up for myself. But even after that beautiful start, I was still afraid to fully claim it as a part of my identity.

I had already put it in my Instagram bio. That was the first quiet declaration to myself. But even then, if someone asked me face to face, I wouldn't say it. It was like, if they see it in the bio, cool—but I'm not claiming it with my mouth yet. Until I did.

It was August 2024. I had just moved to Atlanta and went to my first red-carpet premiere. I met a woman there who asked what I did, and I told her, "I'm a writer." She asked if I was published, and I said, "Not yet." And in that moment, I got the ick. Like, this is why I never say it. Because people will ask for proof. And I didn't have it. I used to think I couldn't call myself a writer until I had accolades. Until I had notches on my belt. But I was in the room. I was in the environment. I had written scripts by then. Maybe they hadn't gone anywhere yet—but they existed.

So I said it. I said it out loud.

The Understanding

When I think back now, I realize—I was never waiting for the world. I was waiting for me.

What helped me realize this was that the affirmations I had long hoped for eventually did come—from people who were already doing this thing. People with résumés and accolades of their own. People who had nothing to gain from gassing me up. Like my professors.

I'll never forget my senior year of college. We were assigned to pitch treatments—essentially, synopses of script ideas—for a group project. Everyone submitted one, and although we ended up using someone else's, the professor—who was notoriously hard to impress—called out mine as the one he was most captivated by. He said it out loud, in front of everyone. And it meant something.

And then there was another professor, in a different class I loved—but I never spoke. I was quiet. Present. Always there, but silent. Then, one day, we watched a film that lit something in me. I finally spoke. After class, he pulled me aside and told me I was brilliant. He said he wished he'd heard more from me all semester.

Those moments of recognition felt good. Great even. But what I came to understand is that even those affirmations, as good as they felt, were only reflecting what was already true. They weren't unlocking something in me. They were just witnessing it. Naming it. Echoing back what I had already known in my spirit for years.

So no—it wasn't them I was waiting on. It was me. Because even before I had scripts to submit to executive producers... I wasn't a writer who never wrote. I was writing all the time. Just not intentionally. Not publicly. Not boldly. But I was writing.

Now, I understand that identity is not about accolades. It's about alignment. It's about honoring what God placed in you before the world ever confirms it. And the writer in me? She was always there. I just hadn't chosen her out loud.

I don't need to perform for proof. I don't need to be celebrated to be valid. The proof isn't the goal—the creation is. The expression is. Obedience is. Because when God places something inside of you, that calling exists whether you walk in it or not. But when you do walk in it, something unlocks.

What makes me a writer is the fact that I kept going. That I still have something to say. That I honor the gift even when no one's clapping. That I chose myself.

So to anyone who's holding a calling in silence—waiting for it to be official—I want to ask you what I had to ask myself:

Are you truly waiting on validation? Or are you just afraid to own it before the world applauds it? Because I didn't need the world's applause. I needed my own permission. And now that I've given it, I have to keep going.

Chapter 3: The Gray Area of Expectations

Learning to Navigate Your Gift When You're Gifted

The Unpacking

I think the weight of being "the strong one" or the one who could just "figure things out" really started with expectations. Not the kind where people explicitly tell you what they expect. But the kind that shows up through what isn't said. What isn't checked on. What isn't offered.

As a kid, I was the one people didn't have to worry about. Or at least, that's what they told themselves. I remember things like never being asked for my report card—not because I was hiding anything, but because my parents just assumed I had it under control. And for the most part, I did. But I'll never forget one semester in middle school where my grades weren't great—like C-average. And still, nobody asked.

At the time, I definitely took advantage of that, but even in the middle of doing it, I remember thinking... Why is this allowed? Like, even if you trust me, I'm still a kid. Shouldn't there still be a check-in? A "let me see how you're really doing?" Something? But there wasn't. Because I was trusted to take care of it. That trust felt like freedom. But it also felt like isolation.

It was the same story with homework. Nobody told me to sit down and finish it. Nobody hovered. Nobody double-checked. I was just... expected to handle it. Because I always had. And yeah, I was responsible. I was smart. I was mature. I cared about school. But I was also a child with emotions, trauma, fears. There were things going on in my life that should've been noticed. Should've been addressed. And emotionally? Mentally? I was carrying way more than a child should've had to.

There were days I cried all the time at school instead of at home. And I'll never forget wishing—hoping—that someone would say something. That a teacher or a counselor or somebody would advocate for me. That they'd call home. That they'd say, "hey, I don't know what's going on, but she seems like she's having a hard time. Maybe check in?" But it never happened. And it wasn't that I didn't have people who loved me. It wasn't that there was no support at all.

But I had become the kid people didn't worry about. The one who could "handle it."

Even my uncle told my dad once, "You don't have to worry about Joi." And I remember that stinging. Because I knew he meant it as a compliment. But all I could think was... if you only knew how often I wished someone would worry about me.

Then there were the compliments. "You're so wise beyond your years." "So mature for your age." I've heard that probably more than anything else in my life. If I got paid every time, I'd be rich. And sometimes, it genuinely feels good coming from certain people, but when it comes from people who haven't shown up—who haven't made space for the parts of me that needed more? The parts that weren't mature? The parts that were struggling? That compliment doesn't land the same. Sometimes, it just feels like another way of saying, "You didn't need what other kids needed." And I did. I really did.

That treatment also felt like, because they expected me to perform well, there was no room for messing up. But I'm human, so obviously I did. The first time I really felt the shift—like people started looking at me differently because I made a mistake—was when I did something I never saw myself doing. Having an abortion.

That may not have been the first time I "messed up," but it was the biggest. And I went through a lot of my darkest moments alone. I didn't tell my parents. I made the appointment. I found a way to pay for it. I got there. I took the medication. I had help from my ex-boyfriend (the dad) and the close friends I trusted, but it was still one of the loneliest, most life-altering experiences I've ever had. And it happened just two weeks before I moved away for college.

So not only did I go through it, I did it right before uprooting my entire life—before being two hours away from everything and everyone I knew. That summer was one of the most depressing times of my life. And the worst part? Even when I did decide to ask for help, I couldn't bring myself to be fully honest. I reached out to a friend from college—someone I trusted—and told her I needed her to pick up my prescription. But I said it was for a miscarriage, not an abortion.

She didn't even know me that well. So why was I so worried about what she'd think? Because I carried those expectations with me everywhere. Even into spaces where nobody had even set them. I couldn't bring myself to admit to doing such a thing. The shame was that deep.

I isolated myself that entire summer. Missed events. Skipped mandatory programs. Wrote makeup papers instead of showing up. I was ashamed. I was angry. And when my parents did eventually find out, it wasn't because I told them—it was because someone I trusted used my truth to take the spotlight off themselves.

They exposed me to prove I wasn't perfect. To prove I wasn't the golden child. And all I could think was... who said I was? It wasn't me. So after already being held to these impossible standards, I also got punished for falling short of them—and again for not wanting to be held to them in the first place.

That whole experience made me resent the very thing people called a gift. And years later, when I got on birth control pills to try and be "responsible," I ended up in the ICU.

My sophomore year of college, first semester, I was actually in a good place. No more depression. A solid group of friends. My first apartment. I had a two-bedroom all to myself—at first, anyway. Later I got a roommate. But during that time, I was living well. I had my space. I had peace. What I didn't know was that the extra bedroom was about to become the place my mom would sleep while she nursed me back to health after I almost lost my life.

I was walking to class one day and suddenly I couldn't breathe. Just a few steps in, and my chest felt tight. I went to class anyway, but I couldn't stay. I got up, walked to the campus health center—having to stop along the way just to catch my breath. I met with my primary care doctor at the time, Dr. Parvaz. Sweetest woman. Small in stature but smart and direct. She ran a quick exam and said the only thing she could think of was a pulmonary embolism—blood clots in the lungs. I immediately started crying. And she tried to reassure me like, "No no no, I'm not saying that's what it is—it's just the only thing I can think of right now." But I knew. If that was the only thing she could think of... that's what it had to be. Something was very wrong with my body.

They sent me to the ER—but it was a record-breaking day. It was packed. I sat for hours in that waiting room, not knowing I was literally at risk of dying. Because when I was sitting still, I felt okay. The shortness of breath only showed up when I moved. So I thought I could wait. I finally got seen. They did a CT scan. And sure enough—several blood clots. One large. Several small. They said if I hadn't come in... that could've been it.

I was 19 years old.

They admitted me immediately, and sent me to the ICU. And because the adult side was full, I got placed in the children's wing. That's how young I was.

The ICU was intense. Everything moved fast in the scariest way. I had to be bathed in my bed by the nurses. It was uncomfortable. It was intimidating. It was too much. I couldn't even call my parents. My closest friend at the time had to make the call. My dad had to drive my mom because she was too emotional to drive herself. And just like that, my entire life changed.

Twice a week, I was getting blood work. Giving myself shots in the stomach. Adjusting my diet constantly based on lab results. All while trying to keep up with school at The University of Michigan, which is not an easy place to be. My mom stayed with me for a week in that extra bedroom. Made sure I was okay. Then she left. And I was on my own again.

That whole experience? I saw it as punishment. Because I felt like the first time—when I got pregnant—it was due to ignorance, carelessness. So this time, I tried to be responsible. I got on birth control. I listened to medical advice. And still, I ended up in the ICU.

And to make matters worse, I was told by the provider that I could skip the placebo pills and take my birth control continuously to avoid a period—because my periods were extreme. But what I wasn't told was how that could spike my estrogen levels and raise the risk of blood clots. And I definitely wasn't told that it would impact future pregnancies. So imagine my surprise when, years later during my first real doctor's appointment after finding out I was pregnant with my son, I was told I was automatically high risk. That I'd need blood thinners for the entirety of my pregnancy. That the same shots I gave myself years ago? I'd have to do that again. With the same ugly bruises and the same depression that came with it.

And it didn't stop there. More problems arose during my pregnancy. Something was wrong, but doctors weren't able to determine what. Not while I was carrying my child. I was going to appointments twice a week, having procedures, and eventually had to be induced prematurely. A few days after birth, my son Casyn was diagnosed with Prune Belly Syndrome—a condition that affects just 1 in every 30,000 to 40,000 children. And all I could think was... I don't win raffles. I don't win giveaways. I've been in rooms with 20 people and my name doesn't get picked. So how did I become the parent of the one in 40,000?

So yes. When I later found out about my son's health conditions—when I learned about his diagnosis—my mind went right back to those clots. That trauma. That fear. That sense of punishment. Was God still mad at me? Had I let Him down so badly that now He was punishing my child for my unmet expectations? The thought passed quickly. But it passed through me all the same.

Still, when I think about Casyn's health, it does connect to this chapter because, though the thoughts of punishment passed, Casyn's health still felt relative to the high expectations I felt were always put on me. I had always believed—long before I became a mom—that my child would come with some sort of challenge. Something rare. Something hard. And I never said it out loud. I intentionally didn't. Because I didn't want to speak it into existence. But I knew.

I didn't know what the challenge would be. Autism? A physical disability? Something else? And I used to think that maybe—if I didn't admit how strong I was—God wouldn't give me something that required strength. Because that's how I felt about a lot of things. Like maybe, just maybe, if I didn't raise my hand, God wouldn't call on me. But He did.

I questioned why God made me into someone who could handle this. I didn't want it. Because it wasn't just about the challenge. It was about what that challenge would cost. About how it would drain me and demand things from me that I wasn't always sure I could give. But deep down... I knew why he chose me. God trusted me. But still, why?

And honestly, that trust is a gift. But it's also a weight. It's being the chosen one when you don't want to be. It's knowing you can carry it, but resenting the fact that you have to. Because it wasn't just a role. It felt like my identity. I felt as though I couldn't get away from those high expectations to perform well and take hits with ease.

And that's where the tension lives.

Then to make the load just a bit heavier, not only was I expected to do well, not only did I often go unnoticed when hard times were overwhelming me, but I was also the glue in so many instances throughout my life as well. The one who kept things light when they felt heavy. The one who could sense discomfort in the air and smooth it out before it turned into awkwardness. I don't know what to call that gift—but I've always had it.

So what happens when the very thing you're praised for becomes the thing that's draining you? What do you do when you know you're gifted, and you understand that you're trusted—but sometimes you don't want to be the one who has to carry it just because you're able? How do you navigate that gift? How do I learn not to resent it—when it comes with so much, and takes so much out of me?

That's when I had to start sitting in the gray. Because this situation was not black or white. It was layered. Complex. Nuanced. It was something I had to make peace with—if I ever wanted to feel free.

The Understanding

So when the weight of it all started to wear on me—when being the glue started to exhaust me instead of inspire me—I realized I had to make a change. And the only way I could do that was through self-awareness.

This is one of the many moments in life where my self-awareness saved me. Because when the problem is something within you, and you trust yourself to fix it, you're not at the mercy of anyone else. You can move on your own time. You're not waiting for someone else to give you a solution. You are the solution. That's what I had to lean into. Because the old ways of thinking weren't working anymore.

It wasn't as simple as, "well, just ignore the gift if it's draining you." That left me feeling unsettled, like I was denying who I truly am—and denying what God placed in me. That didn't feel like freedom. That felt like suppression. But the opposite didn't feel right either. Just giving in fully, embracing the gift with no boundaries, constantly being the strong one, the dependable one, the caretaker? That drained me. That depleted me. That left me running on fumes.

So where was the middle ground? The gray. That's what I had to find.

And I'm still learning. I recently had a conversation with a family friend where I told her how people's expectations have caused me to suffer and she said, "please take this the way I intend it—I don't want you to use that as a crutch," it stuck with me. She wasn't minimizing my feelings. She was holding me accountable for my own life and reminding me that those high expectations were never meant to erase my right to fall apart. They were a reflection of how much people believed in me. And that belief didn't come with the expectation of perfection—it came with the recognition of my gift.

I realized I wasn't waiting on anyone else to give me permission to not always be the strong one—once again, I was waiting on permission from myself. And I had always had the power to give it. Plus, even if some people did put me on a pedestal and expect perfection... So what? Who were they? Why was I abiding by that? The permission to mess up was always there. I just had to grant it to myself.

And grace? Grace didn't have to come from every single person in my life. Some family members may not have realized they weren't extending it. But I've always had people who did. Friends who said, "it's okay to fall apart." Family members who said, "You don't have to have it all together."

So when I think about all the times I rejected that grace—tensed up when it was offered—it makes me check myself. Because if I keep asking for permission to rest, and then resist it every time someone tries to give it to me... maybe the problem isn't them. Maybe it's me. Maybe I've been doing this to myself. And once I realized that, I started to learn how to self-preserve. How to say, "I don't have it in me right now." How to put things down and trust that the people around me could figure it out.

I stopped being the glue in my friend group. I stopped being the one who always had to plan everything. And you know what? Some things did fall apart. But the relationships that mattered? They held. Because the people who were truly connected—outside of me—showed up for each other even when I wasn't the one holding it all together. And that's how it should be.

Sometimes people are willing to help. But if you always jump to do everything first, they'll let you. And then you'll feel unsupported, when really, you never gave anyone the chance. I had to take ownership of the role I played in my own exhaustion. And when I did, I felt so much peace.

The best part? I didn't lose anything important. I'm still the strong one. I'm still the chosen one. I still carry a lot. But I take care of myself now. I check in. I rest. I pause. I preserve. I give myself grace and love. That, for me, looks like stopping and asking, "what do you need in this moment?" Taking everyone else out of it. That's how I check in. And sometimes, when I'm slipping back into old patterns—like I did recently—it helps to have someone model that grace for me.

This season of my life has been heavy. I lost a friend. My dad is extremely sick. I'd been pulled away from home for almost two months. I had to leave work. I was carrying so much. And the stress of needing help—from people who do show up for me—was eating me up. I had to confess how overwhelmed I was to my best friend, and she did exactly what I needed. She modeled grace. She reminded me that I'm allowed to receive. That I don't always have to be the one giving.

That moment helped me give grace to myself. And when I do that? When I take care of me the way I take care of everyone else? I feel light. I feel whole. I dance around my house. I sing. I breathe deeper. I show up better.

But I know what it feels like when I'm slipping. Anxiety creeps in—something I used to experience at extreme levels. My energy crashes. My body aches no matter how much I rest. My signs are physical. They always have been. So now, I try to catch those signs before they escalate and remind myself that I am not any less exceptional when I show up less than perfect.

And if I could talk to the little girl who first believed she had to earn love or value by being exceptional, I would tell her:

You are enough in every state. Every emotional state. Every physical and mental state. Whether you're excelling or "failing" you are always enough. You have always been enough. And you will always be enough. God created you. He knew what He was doing. He didn't miss anything. He didn't mess up the recipe.

So whether you're falling apart or putting someone else back together—you're worth the same. Your self-worth is not based on what you can do. It's not based on how well you perform. But don't forget to excel when you're able to. Because you are able. You are special. So honor that. Just don't let it be the thing that breaks you.

And for the ones out there who are always trusted, always seen as the strong one, always praised for holding it all together... I see you. I am you.

And I want to remind you of this:

Yes, God made you capable. Yes, He gave you strength. But He did not make you God. There may be times where you feel like the strongest person in the room. But you're not—not when God is in the room. And He's in every room. So when it's too heavy, give it to Him. You were never meant to carry it all anyway.

Let Him be who He is—so you can rest in who you are.

Chapter 4: The Gray Area of Grief

Learning to Mourn the Living, the Versions, and the Visions

The Unpacking

Grief is one of those things I used to think was simple. Straightforward. It meant someone died and you were hurting. That was it. That was the definition. At least that's what I believed as a kid. You were sad, someone died, and that was the only story that grief ever told. But then life started happening. Real life. Complex life. And suddenly grief started showing up in spaces where nobody had died—but something still felt gone. Something still hurts. Something still had to be mourned.

I've come to learn that grief is about more than loss of life. Sometimes, it's about the death of an idea, a version of yourself, or a version of the future that never even came to be.

For me, I had to grieve the family I thought I'd have. The life I thought I was building with the father of my child. I imagined doing it "right"—creating a healthy love, breaking generational cycles, and raising children who belonged to both of us. And it wasn't because I was anti blended family. Not at all. My family is a beautiful blended family. I have four brothers and two sisters. I'm the only child between my mom and dad, but you'd never know that unless someone told you. We don't say "half-brother" and "half-sister" or "step brother" and "step sister." We're just siblings. We're family. And even with the ups and downs that come with any big family dynamic, I've always admired the way my mom stepped up for kids that weren't biologically hers, and the way my dad stepped up for kids that weren't biologically his. That shaped me. That showed me what love could look like when it chooses you, not just when it births you.

So no, I never grew up wishing my family looked different. But even in that love, I've seen the complications. The tension. The emotional wars that sometimes come from having so many different relationships and histories all tangled together. So I did grow up dreaming of doing it differently when it was my turn. If it were up to me, I wanted to share all of my children with one man, if he was the man for me. And for a while, I thought I'd found that. I thought we would travel the world together, build a legacy together, raise our son and maybe even one or two more kids. I was dreaming of a united family, a healed partnership, a love that was rooted in intentionality and growth. So when that ended, I had to grieve that too. And it wasn't just the relationship. It was the vision that died with it.

I tried so hard to keep that vision alive after our breakup. We even tried therapy. I was so committed to the idea of keeping it together, not just for us, but for our child. It felt like this massive, monumental thing I could do for him—to give him the family I had always dreamed of building. But eventually, reality caught up to me. And I had to grieve what I had lost, even if it was just a dream.

The moment I knew that vision was truly gone—the moment I really felt it all fall apart—wasn't even necessarily the break up, because there was always the opportunity to get back together. But it was during our time apart, when I found out my son's father had another child with someone else that the vision truly died. And let me be clear: this is not about that child. I would never look at another child as a mistake or an inconvenience. But for me, in that moment, it was like... even if we ever find our way back to each other, it will never be what I originally imagined. The story I wrote in my head for how our family would be—it had already changed. Irreversibly. And so I had to mourn it. Mourn the version of our future that would never exist.

Then there's the version of myself I've grieved too. Or should I say, the versions. The me who didn't know who she was. The me who was always dreaming but never had direction. The me who didn't know how to love herself, or even believe she deserved love in the first place.

If I had to give them names, those are the ones I grieve the most. Because while I'm proud of who I am now, and grateful for who I've become, those girls didn't get the love they deserved when they were here. And I can't go back and give it to them.

And then... there's the grief that this chapter is mostly about. The one I've known longest. The one that's always been there, standing right next to me. The grief I carry for a death that hasn't even happened yet: my dad's.

My father has been sick my entire life. I've been preparing for his death since I was old enough to understand what sickness meant. And I've tried to explain this to people before, but the best way I can paint the picture is this:

There's this hypothetical club people talk about when they lose a parent. The Dead Dad's Club. That's what people call it. And in my mind, I always picture it like a literal club. There are people who are already inside, dancing. Not literally dancing because they're happy about it, but figuratively because they've already accepted it—they're living in it. Then there are people on the complete opposite side of town, not even thinking about that club, because, as far as they know, it's so far away from their reality. And then there's me. I've been standing at the door of that club my whole life. Right by the bouncer. I've never walked in, but I've been too close for too long to pretend it's not real.

There have even been times where I thought I was going to step inside—where the door opened and I braced myself, but then I got pushed back out. That's how it feels every time my dad's health takes a turn and we think, "this might be it." But then it's not. He fights his way back. He survives again. And I celebrate that, I do. But the emotional whiplash of that cycle... It's a lot.

And because I've lived so close to that door, I've done things that people my age usually don't think about. Like the time I asked my dad to walk with me for Homecoming Court. I was a senior in high school. My boyfriend at the time had graduated, and I didn't want to walk with another guy. My dad had just gotten his leg amputated, and I knew how much he loved to dress up—how much fashion meant to him. He hadn't had a reason to get fully dressed in a while. And I thought, "this is the moment." This could be the moment that makes up for him not walking me down the aisle someday, if that day never comes. And so he walked me. And it was beautiful. One of the best decisions I ever made. And I won Homecoming Queen, too—and the votes were already in before we walked, so nobody could say it was a sympathy win. It was just... right.

And dressing up is just one of the few things he loves most. Cooking is another. We used to cook together sometimes. I'll never forget—my dad had all these cookbooks, and honestly, some of them were just for show. Kitchen decor. But one time, we randomly decided to actually use one, and we made a dessert from it. I can't even remember exactly what it was—I just know it had pecans in it and it was so good. We let other people try it, and they were obsessed. To this day, my dad still brings it up. I don't even know if we'll ever be able to recreate it, but it's one of those memories that just sticks with me.

See, the thing is, our family wasn't traditional. It wasn't like, Dad goes to work and Mom stays home. Because of my dad's health, it was the opposite—my mom worked, and my dad stayed home and cooked. She was the holiday soul food cook, but everything else? That was him. And I thought that was so cool.

He used to make the best brownies too when I was younger. All my friends loved coming over—not just for his food, but because they knew dessert meant brownies. Those are some moments I'll never forget.

I'm grateful for those times, I don't ever take them for granted, but having to live like this? To think of moments as simple as cooking together or him making brownies for my friends as potentially being the last? To constantly prepare for what life will be without someone you love that deeply? It's hard. Especially when they keep surviving, and you realize how much life you've lived bracing for something that hasn't even happened yet.

And then there's the grief of the childhood I didn't get to have. Because of my dad's health, there were so many moments I spent in hospitals. I've called 911 more times than a kid should. I remember the reason I memorized his birthday. It wasn't from celebrating it, but because I had to give it to paramedics when his blood sugar dropped dangerously low and he was too incoherent to tell them himself. I've missed out on things. I've spent Christmas and New Year's crying because he was hospitalized. I got blackout drunk at a young age because I was overwhelmed with sadness. I lost my virginity during one of his hospitalizations—when I was home alone, leaning heavily on my boyfriend at the time for comfort. And no, that's not to say I wouldn't have made that decision anyway. But the emotional circumstances absolutely played a part in how and when it happened.

And yet, I want to be clear: I've never blamed my dad for this. I've never looked at my peers and thought, "Wow, they got to be kids in a way I didn't." Not when I was young. Because my dad, despite everything, was present. He came to my games. My school events. My ice cream socials. Sometimes he was the only parent who could make it if my mom was at work. He was there—and I never took that for granted. So it wasn't until adulthood, when I started seeing people my age with healthy dads—dads who can still walk them down the aisle, who'll get to play with their grandkids and watch them grow into adults or go on adventurous family vacations—that I started feeling that ache. That wish for a reality that many medical professionals have predicted I won't have.

I've also spent a significant amount of time simply grieving experiences that his health has stolen from him. Like the vacation we took to Dallas to visit family when I was in middle school. My dad got sick while we were there and spent the entire trip in the hospital. I remember him later saying how he never even got to experience Dallas. And it just stuck with me. Like, wow, this can happen even on vacation. It's not fair.

And now, it's gotten harder. My dad has started to say out loud that he's tired. That he doesn't want to fight much longer. That the will to live isn't what it used to be. And hearing that from him? Digesting that? Trying to respect it, even when it breaks my heart? It's one of the hardest things I've ever had to do.

His illness created an entire environment that I had to survive inside of.

And I'll be honest—sometimes, even his survival comes with grief. I've had to wrestle with gratitude and guilt living side by side. I am immensely grateful that my dad continues to live. That he's fought through impossible odds. That I get to keep loving him in real time. But I'd be lying if I said I wasn't tired. There's emotional damage that comes with standing at the door of that club for so long. It's bracing for an impact that never comes—feeling your body, your heart, your nervous system prepare itself for a loss that almost happened... but didn't. And it takes so long to come down from that. And just when I finally settle, the door cracks open again. Another scare. Another crisis. Another moment that says, "maybe this is it." And then it's not. And I go through the cycle all over again.

So yes, I am grateful. But I'm also exhausted. And that's the gray.

The Understanding

As tough as all of these grieving processes have been, I am first and foremost grateful to just simply be able to articulate what it is that I've experienced. There's a certain kind of peace and healing that comes with being able to name what you've gone through and what you are continuing to go through. And now I know that grief is not as black and white as I originally thought. Although it's not fun to experience, at least sitting in the gray helped me understand the complexities of grief—how it can show up, where it can show up, and why it can show up. And when that's what I'm experiencing, I can name that. I can express that. And like I said, there's peace and healing in that. It allows me to help others identify their emotions and their experiences—those who are where I was, when I didn't understand how complex grief could be.

I now know how to assess how I need to show up for myself because I know what I'm going through. And knowing what I'm going through helps me identify what I need. And once I identify what I need at that moment, I give it to myself. As simple as that. It's not a simple process, but it is a simpler concept, if that makes sense.

Simply experiencing grief and being in it—leaning into it instead of trying to avoid it—has taught me that grief isn't linear.

And also that my grieving doesn't have to make sense to anyone else. It doesn't have to look like anyone else expects it to. I always attempt to make room for joy in the midst of grief.

So when it comes to my son's father and the vision I lost there, that was a tough loss for me to take. But I learned so much from that relationship. I often refer to it as a "trial marriage." It taught me so much about love, about companionship, about family, about responsibility, about stability—and about myself. And it's made me a better parent. It's made us better co-parents. We have an amazing relationship now just as co-parents because of what we learned from what we experienced. And I appreciate that.

The family that we gained from it—and that we're able to give our son—is beautiful. He has amazing family members on my side and his dad's side. And while yes, I still grieve the vision of raising all my children with one man, I still try to see the beauty in everything, because there is beauty in all of it, no matter how things turn out.

That relationship also taught me something else: I was living too far in the past and often too far in the future. I wasn't present enough. I wasn't showing up as the version of me that had the opportunity to exist in that moment. I was either trying to recreate a past that no longer existed or fast-forwarding into a future that hadn't happened yet. And I had to tell myself: be where your feet are. All you have is now. That lesson alone changed how I love, how I process, and how I grieve.

Same with grieving the old versions of myself. Some of it is even laughable—decisions I made, or moments of carelessness that didn't cost me too much. There are things I wouldn't carry into my future, but I'm still able to be appreciative of that time. I can love those versions of myself from where I am now. I accept that I can't go back and love them in real time, But what I can do is honor them. I can welcome back the parts of them that still serve me—the pieces of their fire, their curiosity, their softness—that can live inside the healed version of me. If it aligns with who I believe God called me to be, I'll take it back with open arms. Those versions of me were a crucial part of my journey.

And then with my dad—just being able to recall all these memories, and give him his flowers for the father that he was through all that he was going through—there's a sweetness in that. He taught me so much. And I can see the strength and resilience that he instilled in me, and I can see how it shows up in my own parenting. I pull from his playbook all the time when it comes to encouraging my son. Especially because my son has his own health battles. When he's of age to understand what's going on, I will have a beautiful example of how to guide him because I've seen it modeled.

What I want to remember about the girl who had to grieve her father while he was still here is this: I'm proud of you. I'm proud of you for carrying on through all that pain and all that hurt. I'm proud of you for embracing the memories you were able to share with your father. I'm proud of you for creating those big memories—those core memories. Like the moment you walked for Homecoming Court with your dad. Even if it felt unfair, and like you shouldn't have had to do that, I'm proud of you for doing it anyway. You needed that. You deserved to have that to hold onto. Whether your dad lives to see you get married or not, that memory cannot be taken from you. And that's a beautiful thing. So good job. I know it wasn't easy, but you handled it well.

Anticipatory grief has definitely shaped how I love. It has challenged me and encouraged me to be present, to be forward and vocal about my love. Which is definitely something I need, because I sometimes struggle with being open and honest and forward when I'm in a space of fear and vulnerability (which is why there's a chapter on vulnerability). But living life on that edge—always expecting that moment to come—has reminded me that nobody knows when it's going to come. Even people in perfectly good health could be living in their last days and not know it. So the key is to be present. The key is to acknowledge the now. You've been blessed with this very moment—so live in it. Don't take it for granted. Because no one has promised you another one.

Release, when it comes to grief, is just another form of being vulnerable. It's not pretending it doesn't hurt. It's not pretending I'm so strong that I don't feel what's happening around me, or that I'm not affected by it. It's breaking down when I need to break down. Letting my emotions flow. Naming them. Allowing them to be real and to exist. Sitting in them for as long as I need to—until it passes.

All of these losses also taught me the art of detachment. Not coldness, not avoidance—but true detachment. The ability to stay grounded in the moment, to be fully grateful for the time I have with people, places, and experiences, while also knowing that they may not always be mine to keep. And when it's time to let go, I now know how to do that without losing myself. That's what grief has taught me. That's what the gray revealed.

And as for what God was teaching me through a lifetime of proximity to grief? I think He was teaching me that tomorrow is never promised. And that His people are not ours to keep. My dad doesn't just belong to me—he belongs to God. And whenever God is ready to take him back, He can do that. But even in that, I'm reminded of how good God is. For allowing me to experience my father this long. For letting him live through things that doctors said he wasn't going to live through. For answering my dad's prayer to let him live long enough to raise his children. And then going beyond that—and letting him see his children raise their children.

It's deepened my appreciation for God and what He's done for me and my family. And it's deepened my capacity to feel. I used to think grief was simple. But now I know better. Now I know that grief has layers. And so does love. And sitting in the gray is what helps me hold both.

Chapter 5: The Gray Area of Alignment

Redefining Peace, Success, and Wholeness

The Unpacking

The interesting thing about alignment is that what you're in alignment with is going to keep changing as you change. Sure, there are core values and characteristics that stay with you for life, and the people or places most connected to those unshakable parts might be around forever. But everything else? Some of it's here for a reason. Some of it's here for a season. And it's not always easy to tell which is which—especially when the season ends without a clear goodbye.

At my lowest—when I was desperately trying to find myself, get to know myself, and then learn how to love her—I felt like I had been stripped down to nothing. Completely undone. And the thing is, that stripping down didn't happen out loud. It was a very private process. But luckily for me, in that low moment, I happened to be in alignment with someone who had always been aligned with me: my sister-in-law. Well, technically, my ex sister-in-law now. But honestly, she's just my sister. That's what she was before, during, and after the marriage that initially connected us.

It just so happened that at that time, we were both in similar spaces. We had both fallen into that same kind of emptiness. And even though this journey was mine—deeply personal—I got to share it with someone I trusted. Because it wasn't easy. Like I said, I had to be stripped down to my core. I had to go back and figure out what parts of me were truly mine, and what parts were formed by the world's imprint on me. I had to sort through it all. Take inventory. Rebuild.

And as I did, certain things stopped being appealing to me. People, places, habits—my spirit literally began to resist them. I would walk into environments or be invited to certain things and immediately feel it in my body. A full rejection. A "this ain't it" kind of feeling. And that made things complicated, because some of the people and places I was falling out of alignment with hadn't actually done anything wrong.

It's one thing to create distance when someone hurts you or crosses a line. But what about when there's no conflict? What about when the energy just isn't aligned anymore? That's harder. Because you don't want to seem like you're judging anyone or placing yourself above them. You don't want anyone to feel discarded. There's a weird guilt that comes with that.

But one thing I'll never forget—something I ironically heard from my ex's mom—is that "everybody can't always go with you." And it's true. Some people aren't meant to walk every part of the journey with you. That was a hard but necessary lesson to learn in that season.

And part of what made it harder was figuring out which exits required an explanation and which didn't. What was I allowed to simply let go of without providing clarity? What did I owe, and to who? It was a mental tug-of-war. Especially when it came to people I genuinely cared about. But I had to be real with myself. I had to let the natural thing happen. I couldn't force something that didn't fit anymore.

The moment I realized I was no longer fully aligned with the version of myself I had been was at the end of the relationship with my child's father. As I stated previously, that was a moment when everything fell apart for me. I no longer had the vision I'd been clinging to. I didn't have direction. I was staring at a blank canvas, and I had no idea what to paint on it. And the reason I didn't know what to paint was because I hadn't taken inventory in a long time. I hadn't checked in with myself. I didn't know where I was, what I wanted, what I needed, or what I was even supposed to be doing anymore.

That blank canvas was bittersweet. It gave me freedom—but it also exposed how lost I really was. And that's when I started to understand alignment. That's when I realized how much of my life had been built around specific outcomes. If I could just chase a certain outcome, I didn't have to question the journey. I could shape my whole identity around that destination. But when that outcome was gone, I had nothing to anchor to.

This was also the season where I had to confront my issues with control. I had to challenge myself to let go—to release the need to orchestrate every little thing. And in doing that, I started to lean more into spiritual alignment. Because if I wasn't going to be in control, somebody had to be. And I needed that somebody to be trustworthy. That somebody, for me, is God.

But trusting God meant building a relationship with Him. And that was another blank canvas I didn't quite know how to approach. I didn't know where to begin. I didn't know what I wanted that relationship to look like. I just knew I needed it. That entire season was like that—full of question marks. Full of things I didn't want anymore, but not yet knowing what I did want. It was an in-between space. An emotional pendulum. One minute I felt peaceful. The next, I felt anxious. One day I felt like I was finally gaining clarity. The next, I was more confused than ever.

I'd be feeling five emotions at once, and it made me feel crazy. Like how could I be feeling peace and anxiety at the same time? Joy and grief at the same time? But that's what realignment looks like in the early stages. It's messy. It's lonely. It's quiet on the outside, but loud in the mind. It's hard to explain to people. Especially because I didn't want to let everyone in. I didn't want to share this version of myself while I was still figuring her out.

So I held that version of me close. She was mine. I didn't let the world see her until I was ready to reintroduce myself. And in that quiet, sacred space, I began learning what alignment really meant.

The Understanding

Now we move into the redoing. The rebirth. The tough part—but tough in a different way. The undoing was hard in a heavy, grief-filled, stressful way. This part? The redoing? It came with anxiety too, but it also came with excitement. It was like... now that I'd made space by letting go of everything that wasn't aligned, I had room to meet the version of me that was.

And I began to appreciate that. I began to appreciate the beginning of the process—even the stripping down—because without that, I wouldn't have made it to the other side, where I get to be reborn.

But the thing about this rebirth is that it's completely different from the first one. The first time, I was born into a family, raised by my parents, and heavily influenced by the people, places, and environments around me. This time, though? I was born to be raised by me. With God's guidance, of course—but I had to parent myself through this. And while that is beautiful, just think about how complex it is to raise yourself.

It's been—and continues to be—an incredibly layered experience. It's unfamiliar. It's scary. I had to start asking myself real questions: What works for me now? What doesn't anymore? Who still aligns with me—and who no longer does? How do I want to spend my time? What brings me joy in this new season? What are my hobbies now? What emotions am I comfortable leaning into, and which ones do I still struggle to name or acknowledge? And more importantly... why? There's always a why. And staying aligned with myself means I have to keep asking it. I have to get to the root. Because only then can I be intentional about how I move forward.

That level of honesty has been both revealing and rewarding. It's taught me how to show up for myself. How to extend more grace to myself. How to become my own friend. How to know me. And in doing that, I've learned that choosing alignment over comfort creates so much room for growth. Because comfort will keep you stuck in what you're used to. But alignment will show you what actually serves you. It'll lead you to who you're called to be—and how you're called to contribute.

And that's a big part of alignment too. It's not just about receiving. It's about giving. About service. Being in alignment with myself has helped me see where I can be an asset, where I can offer value, where I can truly contribute. And in doing that, I honor God. And there is no better feeling than that.

Still, alignment has its gray areas. It's not always black and white. Sometimes the lines get blurred. Sometimes your mind and body respond to familiarity, and not alignment. And that can be confusing. But that's okay. The goal isn't perfection—it's intention. And part of that intention is learning how to give yourself grace. Because sometimes you'll be deeply aligned in one area of your life, while feeling completely off in another. And that can be hard to accept. But it's normal. And that's where patience comes in. That's where understanding and gentleness come in.

If I'm being honest, I'd say that right now—my faith, my creativity, and my friendships are where I'm most in alignment. Romantic relationships and work? That's where I feel the most misaligned. And so right now, I'm in a space where I'm intentionally prioritizing those areas—because I want to experience alignment there too.

But I know this much: alignment is impossible to sustain without healthy boundaries to protect it. You have to learn how to set boundaries—with people, with environments, even with versions of yourself. It's not optional. It's essential.

My spiritual alignment especially has taught me to surrender. I once read a quote that stuck with me so deeply, I made it the lock screen on my phone. It said: "God can do so much more with your surrender than you can do with your control." And it's true. I feel more aligned when I let go. When I hand over the illusion of control and just trust that God's plan for me is better than my own. And the more I put my trust in God, the more I've learned to trust myself. It's a win-win. Because when you know God, you start to know yourself better too.

Alignment has completely redefined how I view success. How I define peace. What wholeness even means to me. Because without alignment? I don't think any of those things truly exist.

So to the version of me who had to let go of good things—not just toxic ones—to protect her alignment: you go, girl. For real. You never have to regret honoring yourself, as long as you do it with grace, love, and respect for yourself and for others.

And a note to anyone currently realigning themselves:

Please understand that when you finally meet this new version of you—when you've poured into them, built them up, created space for them to exist—you might find yourself asking, "But how do I be them?" Because you've never been this person before. You figured out who they are, what they need, what they value—but now you have to figure out how to live as them. And that's not always easy.

Here's how I think about it:

If you know me, you know driving is not my favorite thing. It gives me anxiety. But there's one specific vehicle I've always been super comfortable driving. And stepping into a new one? Even if it's an upgrade? It's tough. You know it'll get you further. You know it's safer. You know it has features that fit your life better now. But you don't know its blind spots yet. You're still learning how long it is in the front so you don't hit anything. You're figuring out which parking spots it fits in. You're adjusting to the size, the handling, the feel.

And in that discomfort, it's easy to want to go back to the car you knew—even if it wasn't built for where you're going. But you have to remember: it was time for the upgrade. So be patient. Learn your way around this new vehicle. Trust the process. And don't forget to enjoy the ride.

Chapter 6: The Gray Area of Change

Correction or Redirection? Learning That Not Everything Needs to Be Undone to Be Transformed

The Unpacking

The beginning stages of change can be so challenging. I've said before that self-awareness is a beautiful thing—and it is—but becoming aware of the parts of yourself that may be holding you back can also be deeply uncomfortable. Especially when those parts are ones you've loved. Or, at the very least, ones you've grown attached to. Letting go of pieces of yourself that feel central to who you are—or that you've simply enjoyed—doesn't happen without resistance. I know that firsthand.

There were three specific things I kept coming back to when I thought about the areas in my life that needed to shift in order for me to evolve. Not just grow—but truly become the version of myself I believe I'm destined to be. And while they may not seem deeply connected on the surface, they all had something in common: they were once survival tools that I started to outgrow.

Those three things were:

1. My way of thinking (and the way I spoke to myself)
2. My pride and ego
3. My overuse of social media

Let's start with my mind. Everything is deep to me. That's just how I'm wired. I've always been someone who feels more grounded when I can sit in the gray—when I'm not forced to choose between black or white, right or wrong, this or that. But as beautiful as that level of nuance can be, it comes with its own set of challenges. My mind takes the scenic route with everything. It's layered. Analytical. Emotional. And at times, that's worked against me.

I've talked myself out of opportunities because I overthought them. I've kept things to myself out of fear that people wouldn't understand them—because not everyone processes the world like I do. If someone doesn't think as deeply, they may miss the intention behind what I'm saying, and that misunderstanding creates a disconnect. And once that disconnect creeps in? Insecurity isn't far behind.

And in the midst of all those deep thoughts, especially when I'd start analyzing myself, I'd sometimes spiral. I'd uncover something about myself that I didn't like—something I wanted to fix—and instead of offering myself understanding, I'd just start tearing myself down. I'd point out what I was doing wrong. I'd talk about what I was costing myself. I'd try to correct myself with cruelty, thinking it was discipline when it was really just self-hate. The voice in my head became mean in the name of accountability. And it wasn't helping. It was just hurting.

Then there's my pride and ego. I can't even say for sure what birthed them so strongly in me, but they've been with me for as long as I can remember. At times, they've protected me. At other times, they've sabotaged me. They've made it hard to be vulnerable in relationships. They've made me petty when I needed to be present. And they've led me to protect things that didn't even need defending—at the cost of my growth and emotional honesty.

And finally, social media. Whew. It has consumed so much of my time—time that could've been poured into my purpose, my peace, my people. And while it might sound surface-level compared to the other two, it's deeper than it looks. Because the way I scroll? It's not mindless. I take things in. I internalize. I draw connections. I apply things to my life. And when the content is negative, I absorb that negativity like a sponge—sometimes without even realizing it. One minute I'm watching a funny reel. The next, I'm spiraling over a quote or a post that triggered something I didn't know was still raw.

And here's where it all overlaps: all three of these "problems" were things I also found beauty in.

My deep thinking? Yes, it's caused me stress. But it's also allowed me to connect with people and ideas on a soul level. It's why I can write the way I do. It's why I can see beneath the surface and get to the root of things. I don't just want the pretty—I want the whole picture, even when it's messy. Even when it hurts. So when it came time to change that part of me, I pushed back. Because I didn't want to lose it. I just wanted to make it work better for me.

My pride and ego? As messy as they've been, they've also kept me from begging for love. They've reminded me of my standards. They've stood up for me when I was too tired to do it myself. So even though I knew I needed to change my relationship with them, I couldn't just throw them away. I needed to redefine them.

And social media? As draining as it's been, it's also given me so much. I've had powerful interactions, made real connections, and found posts that helped me name my feelings when I couldn't find the words. I've discovered creative outlets and spiritual affirmations that fed my soul. So even though I knew I needed to change my relationship with it, I couldn't just cut it off and act like it never offered me anything good.

And that's where I found myself stuck—in that tension between what I needed to change and what I didn't want to lose. That tug-of-war between letting go and holding on. Between correction and redirection.

Eventually, I had to stop avoiding the gray and sit inside of it. I had to ask the hard questions and be honest about what was still serving me, and what wasn't. I had to figure out what needed to be reshaped... and what needed to be released completely. That was the only way I could get to the real win.

The Understanding

After sitting with that tension, I realized: not everything has to be undone. Sometimes what we need is not destruction—it's direction. That's what redirection means to me now. It's about giving a newfound purpose to what already exists. It's not about pretending certain parts of me were never there. It's about giving them a new assignment—one that aligns with my highest self.

But some things do need to be let go. Period.

Like that voice I mentioned earlier—the one that used to be mean. That didn't need taming. It needed silencing. There's no upside to being cruel to yourself. I used to spiral—blaming myself, shaming myself, calling myself stupid. Nothing productive ever came from it. So that's one of those things I corrected completely. I shut that voice up, and I'm proud of how well I did it. That voice doesn't live here anymore.

Instead, I ask myself: Can this serve me? If the answer is no, it needs to be corrected. If the answer is yes—with conditions—that's where redirection comes in. Because redirection asks different questions:

- What can this trait offer me or allow me to offer others?
- How do I practice it differently?
- How can I make it align with the version of me I'm working to become?

I started to notice a pattern: the things I needed to correct were almost always learned behaviors. Things rooted in fear, shame, or survival. They weren't reflections of who I am—just how I adapted. But the things I needed to redirect? Those were mine. Natural. Embedded in me. They just needed to be refined.

From a spiritual lens, correction is letting go of what was never meant to be mine. Redirection is returning to what God originally intended—before life distorted it.

My deep thinking? That was always me. But when it got tangled up with anxiety, it turned destructive. Redirection meant taking it back to its pure form. Using it to build, to connect, to discern—not to spiral.

That same shift happened with ego and social media. I stopped demonizing them and started reclaiming control—realistically. I was born in an era where social media is woven into everything: connection, career, creativity. It's not going anywhere. So I asked myself, How can I use it in a way that honors me?

That's how my "Positive Finsta" was born—a tool, a sanctuary, a space curated for nourishment, not noise. I created it to spend less time on my main Instagram page, which follows news outlets, hometown updates, and content that could expose me to drama, tragedies, or negativity I didn't ask for.

On this positive page, I don't allow anyone to follow me—it's just for me. And I only follow accounts that pour into me: affirmation pages, film accounts, my favorite writers, poetry and scripture pages, daily devotionals, career and opportunity boards, even travel and luxury real estate pages that remind me of what's possible. It's a space that inspires me, calms me, and keeps me grounded in the life I'm creating—not overwhelmed by the one I'm trying to outgrow.

This new redirection mindset shows up in my daily life. I still think deeply, but now I don't let it trap me in a loop. I still have my pride and ego, but I don't let them go unchecked. I still scroll, but now I curate.

And every time I choose redirection over correction, I feel like I'm returning to the version of me God always saw. The untouched version. The rooted version. The one the world tried to bury—but couldn't destroy.

So if you're wrestling with whether something needs to be cut off or just transformed, I hope this helps, because not everything needs to be erased. Some things just need to be reassigned.

Chapter 7: The Gray Area of Vulnerability

Not Allowing Hurt To Keep Me Hidden

The Unpacking

Emotional neglect in childhood was absolutely the earliest experience that made vulnerability feel unsafe—or at the very least, unfamiliar—to me. I didn't know that at the time, of course. But when I look back now, I can clearly see the way that certain moments shaped my understanding of what it meant to open up.

There was a particular traumatic experience I went through when I was younger, and I chose to open up to four different adults about it. Two of them responded in a way that helped me. Their reactions were what I needed. But the other two? They didn't say or do much of anything at all. And unfortunately, those two were the ones I had the highest expectations for. The ones I really thought would show up for me.

I now understand—especially as an adult—that their lack of response wasn't rooted in malice. It was a reflection of their own fear, or confusion, or simply not knowing what to say. But that doesn't mean it didn't hurt. That doesn't mean it didn't plant something in me.

To anyone reading this, here's my advice: if someone comes to you with something vulnerable, and you don't know what to do or say, please know the answer is almost never nothing at all. If you don't have the words, start by just being present. Listening is still doing something. Silence, when someone needs support, can be damaging. Don't let your fear of doing the wrong thing convince you that doing nothing is safer. Because that's how I was left—unsupported in one of the hardest moments of my life. And that's where a harmful idea about vulnerability was born in me.

And I've been battling that idea ever since.

The kicker is... if you had asked me a few years ago whether I struggled with vulnerability, I probably would've told you "no." I've always said I believe there's strength in vulnerability. I preach that. I encourage people to be emotionally open. I welcome deep conversations. I share a lot about myself and my life. So from the outside looking in, it seems like I'm very vulnerable.

But what I've come to realize is this: just because I share things that other people would be terrified to say out loud doesn't automatically mean I'm being vulnerable. True vulnerability, for me, would be sharing the things I'm terrified to say out loud. It's not about what scares other people—it's about what scares me.

That was a huge realization. Because I thought I was being emotionally transparent, when really, I was just sharing the parts of me that I had already made peace with. The parts I knew how to explain. The parts that didn't feel risky. But real vulnerability? That means opening up even when you don't have control over how it's going to be received. And that's something I still struggle with.

Another part that's been tough is this expectation I've placed on myself—where even if I am vulnerable and I don't get what I need from someone, I'll be the one who goes out of my way to understand why they couldn't give it to me. Meanwhile, they haven't gone out of their way to understand what I needed in the first place.

That's what feels so unfair. Because now, not only am I emotionally exposed and disappointed, but I'm also the one doing the extra emotional labor to rationalize their behavior. I'm left depleted, comforting someone who didn't comfort me. Explaining to them why it's okay that they didn't show up for me, when they never tried to figure out how to show up in the first place. And that experience taught me: being vulnerable can sometimes leave you lonelier than before.

It created a deep fear. And it built a cycle. Especially in romantic relationships. I would find myself trying to open up—but only a little. I'd over-explain. I'd try to protect myself even while I was telling the truth. I was saying the thing, but I was bracing for impact the whole time. That's not what safety feels like.

And then I got introduced to a relationship where I was actually emotionally seen. I didn't even have to speak—how I felt was visible. I was paid such close attention that my silence said enough. And that changed me. Because once I experienced what it felt like to be truly seen, truly heard, and truly understood... I realized how deeply I craved that.

Now I find myself longing for it again. But here's the twist: even though I want it, I'm afraid to lean in again. I want to feel that safe again... but I don't want to have to ask for it. I don't want to initiate it. It's like, I want to be emotionally seen—without consent. And I know how wild that sounds. But vulnerability feels that tender for me. It's one of those things I want someone to give me without asking.

There's nothing like someone who can hear what your silence is saying. That's what I want in all of my relationships—romantic, platonic, familial. That's also who I want to be for the people I love. Especially for my child. I want to be the kind of person who can sense what someone needs, even when they don't know how to say it. Because I know firsthand how powerful that is. I know how much it can change your life.

But I'd be lying if I said that being seen doesn't still scare me. Because sometimes, even when I am met with exactly what I need... It's so unfamiliar that it scares me too. To the point that I start sabotaging it.

And that has even shown up in my writing as well. Even though writing is my safest outlet, I've had moments—especially with this book—where I've paused and thought, "I don't know how deep into that I'm willing to go." When I'm screenwriting, it's easier. I can hide behind a character. I can say what I need to say without anyone knowing it's me. But with this? With writing this book? There's no hiding. Every chapter, every word, is a piece of me. And that's terrifying.

Thankfully, I don't struggle with vulnerability as much in my friendships anymore. But there was a time I did—especially when I felt like I was performing, or trying to live up to unspoken expectations. But that's something I've grown out of. I'm grateful that my friendships feel emotionally safe now.

What I wish people understood about vulnerability is this: the actual definition of the word means "susceptible to physical or emotional harm." And while I don't want to define vulnerability solely through that lens, it is part of the reality. When someone is being vulnerable, they're taking a risk. They're giving you access to their tenderest parts. And even if they trust you, there's still liable to be fear there.

So when someone opens up, imagine how much is at stake for them. Think about what it costs. And if you've ever regretted being vulnerable, you know what I mean. Even in moments where I knew I made the right choice, I've still regretted it. Because vulnerability can come with anxiety. It can come with fear. So the second something feels off—if the conversation doesn't go exactly how I believed I needed it to go—I spiral. And I start thinking, "I never should've shared that."

That's the emotional tug-of-war I live with. That's the war inside me when it comes to vulnerability.

The Understanding

I've learned so much about myself through my relationship with vulnerability. For one, I learned which parts of me were actually true, and which were just assumptions I'd made about myself. Like I said, a few years ago, I would've confidently told you that I was a vulnerable person. But now I realize that wasn't really true—not in the way I thought. And even though it was hard to admit, there was something beautiful about learning that. Because once I could be honest with myself about where I was lacking, I could start to grow.

The first step was acknowledging that I hadn't been practicing vulnerability in the way I thought I had. And once I did that, I started doing the work. I'm back in therapy now, and this time, I intentionally chose a Black male therapist. I knew that since my biggest struggles with vulnerability show up in romantic relationships—and those relationships are always with Black men—it made sense for me to intentionally build a different kind of emotional connection with one. This dynamic is obviously different being that it's a professional one, but still, I wanted to let myself be fully seen by a Black man in a space that was safe and healthy. I also knew this would help me navigate some of the emotional tension I've carried in relation to my dad, also a black man.

I know that my dad or not every Black man I date going forward will hold space for me the way my therapist does. I'm not naive about that. But still—it matters. It was a bold and intentional step toward healing. It's also helped me expand my thinking, especially in moments where I confuse discomfort with danger. Because sometimes, when I feel unsafe being vulnerable, it's not that I'm in actual danger—it's that I don't understand the other person's perspective. This space helps me work through that.

Healthy vulnerability for me now looks like showing up with a full cup. If I walk into a situation and I end up being disappointed, it doesn't drain me completely—because I came in full. I still have me. I still have God. But when I was emotionally depleted, when my cup was already empty, and I was hoping someone else would pour into me, the impact of disappointment was so much greater. So now, I take care of myself first. Because yes, people need people—but I also need to be good to myself.

As far as healing through vulnerability, therapy is again a major example. My therapist is helping me understand that I don't have to always be preparing for the worst. I don't have to welcome it. I don't have to expect it. I used to think that expecting disappointment would somehow protect me from it—but all it really did was rob me of peace. I'm learning to shift that.

And then there's this book. Like I mentioned, I constantly asked myself how much I wanted to share and how deep I wanted to go. I knew I couldn't hide. And still, I chose to lean in. I chose to be open. I chose to be honest. I considered the impact that my vulnerability might have on someone else—that it might do more good than harm. And that's what helped me push through.

Then God. God has played the biggest role in my healing. Knowing that He is a constant safe space has made it less scary to risk being open with people. Because I know that people are going to fall short sometimes. They won't always respond the way I need. But that's not always about me. It's not always personal. God's presence reminds me of that. And He reminds me that even when others don't show up, He always will.

I still believe that there's strength in vulnerability. I've preached that to others for years. But now, I finally turn that truth toward myself. Because it takes a strong person to be soft, to be open, to let themselves be seen.

So to the younger version of me who learned that vulnerability wasn't safe:

This isn't black or white. I know you're hurting. I know it didn't feel fair. But two things can be true: you did the right thing by being vulnerable—and the result still hurts. But not everyone will respond that way. And staying closed off to protect yourself will end up costing you more than being vulnerable and disappointed ever will. Don't miss out on something beautiful just because the first time didn't go well. Don't be the reason you never get to experience what it feels like to be safe and open, to be seen, heard, and understood. Because once you feel it, you'll know why it was always worth the risk.

Chapter 8: The Gray Area of Influence

The Risk and Responsibility of Having Something to Say

The Unpacking

I've always felt like I've had something to say.

Whether it's through mentoring, life coaching, screenwriting, public speaking, or even photography and creative projects like documentary filmmaking—I've always been drawn to things that let my voice shine through. Things that allow my perspective to take shape in the world. Even writing this book comes from that place. I know my voice is meaningful. I know what I have to say matters. And I truly believe there's someone out there who needs to hear it.

But sometimes, I still find myself discouraged.

Sometimes I wonder, "Aren't there already enough voices saying what I'm trying to say?" And the truth is, that question has stopped me in my tracks more times than I can count. One example?

I started a podcast with my best friend. We created multiple episodes, had real conversations, poured ourselves into it—and yet, I couldn't bring myself to put it out there. And truthfully? I've never even had this conversation with her. So if you're reading this, surprise.

Part of why I struggled to release those episodes was because I kept thinking: What's so special or unique about what I'm saying? What am I going to say that hasn't already been said?

Even now, I still battle those thoughts. But I know that's fear talking. Or the enemy playing tricks on me. Or just the weight of overthinking. Because the truth is, I've heard things before—words from people like Jay Shetty or Will Smith—that changed me. Not because they were the first to say them. But because of how they said them. When they said them. Where I was in life when I heard them. Those words didn't just change my life. They changed my mind. And I think that's such a powerful thing. To shift someone's perspective just by speaking truth in a way that resonates.

So even if what I'm saying isn't new... it might still be necessary. Maybe it's not about being the only one who says it. Maybe it's about being the one who says it in a way that someone can finally hear. I try to remind myself of that.

It's kind of like how people say, "There's enough money to go around," when talking about doing the same thing as someone else. I try to apply that same thinking to my voice. There's enough room. There's enough space for me, even if others are already out there. But the gray area for me is mixing that truth with my fear. It's the tension between knowing there's room—and still feeling like maybe there isn't.

Another part of it is this: it's not that I want to be understood by everyone. I don't even have the desire for that. But I haven't fully stepped into the place where I feel like my way of thinking is safe for public interpretation. I live in the gray. Like, really live in the gray. And I've only recently realized just how often I do.

There's a phrase that really helped me understand this. One I hear women say to each other all the time: "If he wanted to, he would." It's said as a way to hold men accountable in dating and relationships. But when I heard it, I didn't think about it as the woman. I thought about it from the perspective of the man. What if someone said that about me? "If she wanted to, she would."

And my immediate thought was: But there are so many things I want to do that I don't. Not because I don't care. Not because I don't love deeply. But because of trauma. Because of fear.

Because of anxiety and overwhelm. Because of what I've been through. So it's not always as simple as, "If I didn't do it, it's because I didn't want to."

That's when I realized—my brain just works differently. I don't naturally lean into black-and-white thinking. My whole life lives in nuance. I consider the context. I think about the reasons behind the reasons. I live in the gray.

But living in the gray requires boundaries. It requires self-awareness. It requires accountability. Otherwise, it gets dangerous. Because when you extend too much understanding to people without holding them accountable—or when you make too many excuses for yourself without being honest—you end up excusing harmful behavior. And that's not the kind of influence I want to have on people.

That's why I'm careful. It's not that I don't trust myself—it's that I'm hyper aware of how easily people can twist things. And I do feel a sense of responsibility. Not to control how people interpret every single word I say—but to do my best to make sure I'm not leaving too much room for misunderstanding.

Some things, like "If he wanted to, he would," have their place. Like yeah—if a man knows you love flowers and he doesn't even try? Then maybe it's true. Maybe he just doesn't care. A broke man could still go pick some wildflowers, you know? But that saying doesn't apply to everything. It has a time and a place. And I want to be the kind of person who helps people see that—not just repeat something because it sounds good.

I also want to mention something else that's a big deal for me when it comes to using my voice: I have this deep desire for my messages to be digestible. I can't stand when people use language as a gatekeeping tool. When someone has an extensive vocabulary and uses it like a weapon—intentionally speaking in a way that only a select few can understand—that's a huge turnoff to me. I think intelligence and depth mean being able to make your message accessible.

If you're really brilliant, you should be able to explain your point to an 80-year-old and an 8-year-old. Someone with a doctorate and someone who didn't finish high school. You should be able to speak in a way that doesn't require someone to decode you. Otherwise, who are you really helping?

Yes, I love words. And yes, expanding my vocabulary is something I want to do for myself and for my son. But not to intentionally intimidate others. So I can understand more, not exclude more. The reason I'm even bringing this up is because that's how I want this book to feel. I want it to sound like me. I want to speak how I naturally speak—clearly, intentionally, and with heart—but I don't want the message to only land with a certain kind of reader. I don't want it to only make sense to people with a certain education level or life experience or vocabulary. I truly believe there's something here for everybody. And if what I have to say can only be understood by a select few, then I'm not really saying it in a way that honors the heart of my message. This book isn't about showing how articulate I can be. It's about connecting. And I want every single person who picks it up to feel like they're being talked to, not talked at.

And so yeah—this is what influence looks like for me. This is what it feels like inside my head. The constant tug-of-war between believing I have something meaningful to say... and worrying about how it'll be received. The dance between wanting to be heard... and fearing being misunderstood.

All of these fears—misinterpretation, repetition, trying to get it just right, trying to make sure the message lands perfectly for every demographic—have honestly hindered me. I know it. I've let those fears stop me from creating. From sharing. From releasing things into the world that were already good and ready and full of purpose.

There's so much I could've already produced, so much more I could've shared by now, if I hadn't let the weight of "getting it right" slow me down. And that's the part that frustrates me the most. Because I know I have something to say. I know my voice matters. I know there are people who need it. But somewhere along the way, I started letting the fear of getting it perfect be more powerful than the truth that it was already worthy of being heard. And I know I'm not alone in that. And maybe, just maybe, someone needed to hear that part too.

The Understanding

Now that I've accepted the gray area of influence—the part that doesn't require perfection—I finally feel free to use my voice. And not just use it, but use it boldly. My voice today sounds like me speaking without overthinking. It looks like me showing up and not concerning myself with every possible reaction. It looks like trusting that God will get the message to whoever needs it—and letting go of the rest.

Because I've realized, I can't take responsibility for everyone else's interpretations. If someone hears what I say and decides to twist it, or just doesn't receive it the way I intended, that's not something I can control. And I can't stay silent because of that.

Because then I rob the people who would have received it. I rob myself—because I need to say it. And I rob the message—because it needs to be shared.

This is a space where I'm actively surrendering perfectionism. Because perfectionism has been crippling. It's kept me from creating, from sharing, from producing things that could've already made an impact. I've sat on so many ideas, so many messages, all because I was scared they weren't perfect. But what good does that do for anyone? And how is that honoring the gift I was given?

At the same time, I do still value intentionality. I believe we have to be careful with our words. Especially in a world where "influencer" is a literal job title. Influence is being treated casually—but I don't think it should be. There are young people out here taking in everything we say. So even though I'm working through the fear of misinterpretation, I still believe influence should come with a sense of responsibility. If I want to reach a wider audience someday, I want to do it with care and intention.

What ultimately helped me let go of the pressure to say things perfectly was realizing how not saying anything at all was costing me. It was costing my growth. It was costing my creativity. It was costing my peace. My voice is necessary—even in a world full of voices—because someone out there is specifically waiting to hear it from me.

Maybe they need to hear it from someone who looks like me. Or someone who sounds like me. Or someone who uses the exact vocabulary I use, or who's the same age I am, or who delivers the message through a medium they connect to. All of that matters. Just like the people who've changed my life with their words– maybe I'm meant to do that for someone else. Maybe it's not about saying something no one's ever said before. Maybe it's about saying it in a way they can finally hear.

Had I not sat in the gray and made space for both my fears and my wants, I wouldn't have reached this point. I probably would've kept shutting myself up—or worse, started speaking carelessly just to prove that I could. But now I know better.

So if you're reading this and you know you have something to say: say it. Say it mindfully, say it truthfully, say it with love—but don't silence yourself. Because even if your voice isn't perfect, it's perfect for the ears that need to hear it.

Chapter 9: The Gray Area of Faith & Opportunity

Redefining Success Through Trading Black-and-White Myths for Grayer Truths

The Unpacking

You know how you can be learning something or getting hints of it over time—like something's been brewing under the surface—but then you finally hit a moment where you can name it? Like, out loud? I think that's where I am right now with this idea of believing in my talent but not believing in my opportunity.

For so long, something felt off, like there was a missing piece I couldn't name. But the thing is, I never really felt like I wasn't good enough. That was never the issue. When it comes to the things I love—especially writing—I've never felt like I lacked the talent. I've never looked at my screenwriting and thought, "This isn't worthy of being on TV." I've never thought my name didn't belong in credits or that my stories couldn't change lives or make money. Never.

But something in me still held back. I started amazing things and didn't always finish them—not because I doubted my ability, but because I didn't believe the opportunity would come.

I tried to name it as imposter syndrome, but even that didn't fully fit. I would literally read the definition, thinking, "Maybe this is it," but I knew something was off. It's not that I thought I wasn't deserving of what I had—it's that I didn't believe the next thing was actually going to show up for me.

That truth hit hard when I started pushing myself to really try—to enter contests, pitch to executives, put my work in front of people. Because for a while, I had this safety net of not trying. That way, if nothing happened, I could say it's because I didn't put myself out there. But once I did start trying, and the silence still came? That's when the ache settled in. That's when I realized the gap between what I believe I'm capable of and what I still haven't received.

I'll never forget this one pitch. It was my first one ever, to an executive of a company tied to a major Hollywood name. The executive gave me fives across the board—on a seven-category scorecard. In every single category, a five. His comments said:

"Really well done. You've crafted entry into a deft and compelling world here, fueled by believable character dynamics and a real WHY to the story. This is a rarity. I'd love to read your writing." So I sent him my script.

Nothing. No response.

But what makes it even more complicated is that I didn't just email him directly—I submitted through a platform that requires a follow-up. It's literally built into the program. So it's not even a case where I could just assume, "Oh, he didn't respond, so maybe he hated it." Because if he did read it and did hate it, he's still obligated to respond and give that feedback. That's the way the system works.

And as much as it would sting to hear, "I didn't like your writing," at least I would know. At least I'd be able to say that the opportunity didn't come because it wasn't a fit. But instead, I'm just left in this limbo where I can't even place what went wrong—or if anything went wrong at all. And that just feeds deeper into the feeling that the opportunities I'm expecting... somehow keep slipping through the cracks.

Same with this book. I believe it's going to be amazing. I believe it's powerful. But I don't know if it'll reach the people it's meant to reach. Will people who don't know me read it? Will it find its way into the hands of someone who needs it? I don't know. And that not knowing is exhausting.

Sometimes I look around and think—what do I really have to show for all this belief people have in me? I stay afloat. I take care of myself. I do amazing things. But I still feel like I'm not breaking through. Like none of it is soaring. And that's hard to sit with, because I know my talent isn't the issue.

When I think about that gap between my capability and my reality, my body literally aches. I feel like my life is on pause. I keep ending up on these breaks from 9-to-5 jobs, and I want to believe it's divine timing—that I'm supposed to be focused on what God really called me to do. But nothing shows up in those breaks. I'm willing to work for the opportunity, but I feel stuck in not knowing how.

I saw this video once—it said, "If you knew you were 30 failures away from your dream, how fast would you fail?" And I thought, Fast as heck. But the truth is, I don't even know what direction to fail in. I don't know where to pour. I don't know what's worth trying anymore.

My original plan was to graduate, move to L.A., bust my butt as a PA, and work my way into a writer's room. But life didn't go that way. The pandemic happened. I got pregnant. I started a family. That family fell apart. And only after all that did I start actually writing. Now, I'm trying to lean on contests and mentorships and pitch sessions. And even when I get amazing responses, the next step never seems to come.

Same thing with my coaching business. I know I'm gifted. I know I'm called to this work. I became trauma-informed. I built the foundation. I created a pitch to schools, sent it to people who literally called me out for not asking for their help—and promised to help me push it forward. And then silence.

And then there's the people who believe in me. Like Kay, for example. Kay is—

Kay was...I have to get used to referring to her in the past tense.

But Kay was my very first real college friendship. She rescued me from the kitchen floor of a summer college party I had passed out at. People assumed I was drunk, but I wasn't—I was actually dehydrated. And Kay didn't just check on me, she saved me. We had been friends for nine years after that, until she passed away due to health issues she had been battling.

And as I write this chapter, it's only been three days since I even became aware that she's gone.

The reason Kay comes to mind right now is because... she believed in me. Deeply.

I still have the message from when I let her read my scripts for the first time. She told me she was on the edge of her seat at the cliffhanger. She said she could see it—see the show, see the world I built. She said it felt like she was waiting for next week's episode to drop. And then she had to remind herself it wasn't real yet—that it was something I made up, that lived in my mind. She said she could see my name in the credits.

And now... she's gone.

And as much as it hurts, I know she would tell me to keep going. She was fighting for her degree until the very end. She was supposed to graduate this May. She never stopped trying. And that's where guilt creeps in—because I'm still here. I'm still alive. And if I were to quit now... I don't think I could live with that. It wouldn't just dishonor her—it would dishonor myself. And the God who gave me this gift.

So no, I'm not stopping. It's not motivation I lack. It's direction. It's faith that the arrival is real—that opportunity is still out there for me.

That's what I'm struggling to hold right now.

I think one of the hardest parts of grief is not just missing someone—but realizing what they saw in you, and wondering if you'll ever see it come to life.

Kay saw something in me. Not just talent. Possibility. And for whatever reason, it's that part I struggle to hold onto for myself.

There's something uniquely heavy about being believed in. It should feel like a gift—and it is—but it can also feel like pressure. Especially when you don't know what you have to show for it. When people say, "I know you're going to make it," and you're thinking... But what if I don't? What if they were wrong? Or worse, what if they were right and I just couldn't figure out how to make it happen?

The even trickier part is... their belief in you doesn't come with directions. It doesn't come with steps. It doesn't come with a roadmap, a guide, a "here's how you get there." It's just belief. And while that belief can feel grounding, it can also feel lonely. Because then what? You're sitting there holding this dream, surrounded by people who see it in you... but none of you know how to get there.

That's where the gray is.

That's the part that messes with me. Because I get it. You believe I'm going to make it. I believe I'm going to make it. But how? How do I get to this reality we both see for me in our heads?

I don't doubt my gift. That's the strangest part. I have full confidence in what I create. I believe in the power of my writing, my voice, my presence. I believe I've been called. But what I don't always believe in... is the pathway to that calling being cleared. I don't always believe the opportunity will come. And that's not something we talk about enough.

We hear a lot about people who doubt themselves. But what about the ones who don't? What about the people who do believe in their work, who do show up, who do keep trying—but still feel like doors stay closed for no clear reason?

That's the gray area. The space between confidence and disappointment. Between boldness and delay. Between "I know I'm meant for this" and "but what if I never get the chance?"

The Understanding

I'm learning that this space doesn't mean I'm doing
something wrong. It just means I'm walking a path that's unfamiliar,
undefined, and sometimes unfair. It means I'm having to build faith
not just in what I carry—but in the possibility that the world might
make room for it.

That's a different kind of faith. One that requires me to trust
without evidence. To believe without applause. To keep writing even
when the silence gets louder. To keep creating even when the
breakthrough hasn't come. And sometimes, when I don't have that
belief in myself, I borrow it. I borrow the confidence that Kay had. I
borrow the faith my mentors have. I borrow the eyes of the people
who've seen me clearly and still said, "You're going to make it." I lean
on their certainty when mine runs dry.

There was a message that lived on my whiteboard long before
I ever needed it. I got it from a co-host of a well known podcast I
used to love before it ended. The hosts had lost their friend, and one
of them said their friend's passing made her feel guilty—because her
friend was so full of life and gratitude, and yet it was her life that got
taken. Meanwhile, she was still here, not always feeling that same
level of appreciation. The message was a vow to live more fully and

with more gratitude in honor of her friend. It didn't apply to my life at the time. But for some reason, I wrote it down. And now, after losing Kay, I know exactly why.

So, once again, we're in the gray.. I may be doubting that opportunity will come. But I still have life. And with life, there is still space for opportunity to come.

Kay doesn't have that anymore. That chance was taken from her before she could walk across the stage and finish what she started. And when I reached out to her sister—a woman I had never spoken to before, but who I knew Kay loved deeply—the last line of her message to me was:

"All I ask is that you keep her memory alive and be great. Just like she would have wanted."

That message brought me right back to that quote. It confirmed that it was for me. That I was meant to carry that reminder. And that now, more than ever, I owe it to Kay. I owe it to our friendship. I owe it to myself. And I owe it to God.

And I want to say this to whoever is reading this:

This chapter was written in real time. The first half—the raw conversation—was me literally venting through my grief and frustration. I was writing from the heat of the moment, from uncertainty, from the thick fog of not knowing what to do next. And when I finished writing that part, I took a nap. And when I woke up, I watched a podcast clip. And it shifted something in me. Because in the first part, I mentioned how I've never doubted my talent. And part of the reason why is because people have told me that I've changed their lives. That I've saved their lives. And sitting with that... made me check myself.

How dare I say I've never had opportunities?

Maybe not the big ones I dream of—TV deals, full-time writing jobs, sold-out book tours, a six-figure coaching business. But I have had opportunities. Every time I used my gift to help someone, to shift something in them, to hold space or breathe life into their story—that was an opportunity. An opportunity to walk in my purpose. And I did it.

There may not be a paycheck or a platform attached to those moments. But there was an impact. And that's what I believe God gave me this gift for. The tangible rewards? I still want them. I still pray for them. But I won't ignore what's already happened just because it didn't come with a certain level of recognition.

Saying I haven't had opportunity is only true if I'm looking at life through a black-and-white lens—where success means money, visibility, and scale. But that's not the truth I'm living. That's not the truth I want to live.

When I open myself to a broader perspective—when I widen the lens—I find peace in the gray. Peace that reminds me: God has already been using me. The blessing isn't just coming. It's already shown up. And the more I see that, the more I trust that bigger blessings are still on the way.

Chapter 10: The Gray Area of Proximity

When Growth Creates Distance

The Unpacking

There was a friendship in my life that felt like family. Still does, honestly. Even though we don't talk now, I sometimes catch myself referring to her that way—because for so long, we weren't just close, we were bonded. By choice, not blood. And we stood on that.

But something shifted. And I don't mean suddenly or dramatically—just gradually, over time, in a way I didn't fully notice until I did.

There was one moment I'll never forget. We were together, just the two of us, and I got really quiet. It wasn't planned or heavy. It was just... quiet. But while we sat there, side by side, I remember feeling like I'd never been further away from her. Not physically—energetically. I didn't say anything at the time. I didn't even know what I would've said. But the energy felt off, and my body noticed it before my brain could.

Not long after that, something happened that brought me right back to that moment. I watched her be the version of herself I had just started to sense. But this time, she was being that version with someone else. It was like I had seen the storm clouds forming, and then, right after, it rained—just not on me.

That moment confirmed what I had been feeling. It wasn't just a weird vibe or a passing phase or me overthinking. It was a shift. And I knew then that if I stayed too close, long enough, I might end up in the middle of that same storm. I didn't want that for either of us. I didn't want things to unravel to the point where they couldn't be salvaged. I didn't want to wait until I was angry or bitter or disappointed. I wanted to honor what we had by stepping away before either of us caused real damage. And that's exactly what I did.

I didn't exit with intentional drama. I didn't make a big announcement to anyone outside of her. I just followed what I knew in my spirit: that we weren't in alignment anymore. And that, for now, we needed space.

I wasn't looking to abandon her. I wasn't trying to punish her for being a version of herself I didn't understand. I just knew I couldn't keep showing up the same way I always had when something inside me knew it wasn't the same anymore. And I felt okay about it. Really okay. Which honestly surprised me.

I expected to feel sad. I expected to feel heartbroken. I expected to feel... something more. But I didn't. I didn't feel relief either—I hadn't been miserable in the friendship. I didn't feel trapped before I left and I didn't feel resentment after leaving. I just felt... fine.

And then came the guilt. Not guilty for letting go. Guilty for how NOT sad I was about it. That's what threw me. I had just gone through a completely different kind of heartbreak not long before that, and it tore me up inside. So the fact that this felt so clean, so calm—it made me question myself. Was I in denial? Was I emotionally checked out? Was I dissociating?

But years have gone by. And I still feel that same calm. That same clarity. That same peace.

That emotional contrast between two different kinds of goodbyes? That's another part of what keeps me aware of the importance of the gray. Because if I had been thinking in black and white, I would've assumed that my lack of grief meant I didn't really care. Or that maybe our relationship wasn't as deep as I thought. But that wasn't true. I still loved her. I still do. I just knew that loving her didn't mean we had to stay close. And that's a whole shift in itself.

This time it wasn't anyone else misunderstanding me. I think I misunderstood myself at first. I couldn't figure out why I wasn't grieving something I once held so close. And it made me question if I was cold or emotionally detached. But the truth is, I wasn't detached—I just wasn't sad. I was in full connection with what I was feeling... it just wasn't what I expected to feel.

Even now, I still carry a sense of love and respect for that friendship. One of the things that makes me emotional about it is the fact that we chose each other. We weren't born into each other's lives—we said, "You're my person." And we meant it. We stood on it so fully that it still feels real to me today. Like we're related. Like nothing can undo that.

And because I know how deeply I still love her, I don't question my integrity as a friend. I know how I showed up. I know how intentional I was. I know I didn't leave in avoidance—I left in awareness. I wanted to preserve what we had. And the only way to do that was to stop trying to force it to be something it no longer was.

I had a similar experience with a family member. I got to a place where I realized the kind of relationship I wanted with them just wasn't going to happen. Not because I didn't try—but because I couldn't control who they were or how they saw me. Even when I stopped expecting them to pour into me the way I poured into them—even when I released the idea that our relationship had to be balanced in order to be valid—I still wasn't being respected in the most basic ways. And that's where I drew the line.

I didn't ask for more than what they had the capacity to give. I just asked for the bare minimum: to be heard, to be honored, to have my boundaries respected. And when that couldn't happen, I let go. Not out of bitterness—but out of peace.

I've had my boundaries challenged by this person behind my back. And while it would be easy to let that shake me, I saw it as confirmation that I've become someone whose boundaries are too solid to argue with to my face. And honestly, I'm proud of that.

The Understanding

What surprised me most about both of these situations was how calm I felt throughout. There was no spiral. No resentment. No over-explaining. Just clarity. Just alignment.

The gray area, in this case, was the space between loving someone deeply and still choosing distance. It was realizing that I could care about someone forever and still not foster a relationship with them. That I could hold space for their growth, even from afar. That I could love them without losing myself.

And maybe most importantly, it was realizing that detaching isn't always a sign of coldness or avoidance. Sometimes, it's a sign of clarity. Because while people expect clarity to only come from black or white decisions, this was a perfect example of me finding real, deep clarity by sitting in the gray.

Again, had I only thought in black and white, I might've convinced myself that I didn't love them as much as I thought. Or that I must be faking it—numbing out—because I wasn't hurting more. But neither of those things were true. I just learned that sometimes, when you're in alignment with yourself, peace comes quietly. And when you feel it, you don't need to explain it.

This gray area gave me the clarity I needed—to choose alignment over attachment. Before these shifts happened, I had already gone through the kind of heartbreak that introduced me to unconditional love. So when I walked through the separations that followed—whether with friends or family—I had a new lens. A new understanding.

Because what I realized was this: unconditional love doesn't mean love without boundaries. It means the love still exists, even when the closeness doesn't. And that's how I experienced it. The love didn't stop. But the shape of the relationship changed. The expression of love changed. And that was okay.

Peace showed up for me during these transitions in the softest, most subtle way. It wasn't loud. It didn't announce itself. It just existed in the background. In the silence. In the way I was able to keep living without spiraling. In the way my overthinking never kicked in. My mind—the place that usually holds so much noise—was finally quiet. And that quiet felt like peace.

Still, I had to check in with myself. Because peace didn't feel like the "right" reaction to separation. I expected sadness. I expected loss. I expected to miss them. And when I didn't feel those things, I wondered if something was wrong with me.

But then I realized... guilt, in this case, wasn't signaling wrongdoing. It was signaling conditioning. I had been taught to believe that losing someone you love always results in pain. That choosing distance means something went wrong. That peace only comes after struggle. But that wasn't my truth.

I am in tune with myself enough to recognize the difference between guilt that comes from hurting someone—and guilt that comes from doing something differently than I was taught to. And in these cases, I knew I hadn't done anything wrong. The guilt didn't come with shame. And it didn't stick around long. Because right behind it was peace. And, for me, peace doesn't follow wrongdoing—it follows alignment.

If you're afraid to set boundaries because you associate love with closeness, I'd invite you to reframe the question. Not, "How do I love them and still set this boundary?" but, "What does it look like to love myself right now?" Because sometimes, loving you means choosing distance. And sometimes, choosing distance is the most loving thing you can do for everyone involved. That is how you'll see things when you look through the lens. I'm encouraging you to look through.

That lens continued to serve me later in life. There were two other friendships—ones I never expected to step away from—that eventually required the same kind of separation. And once again, I felt peace instead of sadness. But this time, there was no guilt. No confusion about how I was supposed to feel. Despite what I was originally conditioned to think, I had learned to trust what peace feels like. I had learned to believe in myself.

I believe that detachment can coexist with deep love. Because again, the love itself can be unconditional. The expression of that love is what changes. And that's allowed.

Looking back on these decisions, I'm most proud of how I honored myself—without letting it turn me cold. I still love those people. I still wish them well. I still hold gratitude for the seasons we shared. But I also know that I'm not supposed to stay in places where I'm no longer in alignment. That's not disloyalty. That's integrity.

The gray area challenged my old ideas of loyalty, for sure. It made me realize that starting with myself isn't selfish—it's sacred. And the more I center my own truth, the more I find myself surrounded by the right people. The ones who meet me where I am. The ones who see me clearly. The ones who are growing, too.

Because when I lead with alignment—when I let the gray guide me—I always end up where I'm supposed to be. In close proximity of my peace.

Chapter 11: The Gray Area of Balance

Becoming More for Others Shouldn't Mean Becoming Less for Self

The Unpacking

When I first became a mom, a lot changed.

The best part? I took my mental health more seriously than I ever had before. Almost immediately. Because for once, it wasn't just about me. I could ignore my own needs, delay my own healing—but now there was another human in the picture. One who didn't ask to be here. One who didn't deserve to carry the weight of whatever I hadn't dealt with. So I jumped into therapy with a kind of urgency I probably wouldn't have had if it were just me.

But it wasn't all good change.

There were shifts that didn't feel like growth. Shifts that scared me. Parts of myself that I could feel slipping away—not because I didn't want them, but because I didn't know if they were allowed to stay.

The version of me that was spontaneous. The risk-taker. The girl who could pack a bag and move across the country—or even abroad—on nothing but faith. She always felt bold. Free. Unafraid to fall, because it was just her. But now, there was a child. And suddenly, falling didn't feel like an option.

I didn't know how to let that girl exist in the same world as the version of me who was somebody's mother. And the more I leaned into motherhood, the more I felt her disappearing. I held myself to such a high standard that there was barely room for the "me" I used to be. And while that might sound noble, it didn't feel good in my spirit. I felt off. Like I was living wrong. Like my choices looked right on paper but felt heavy in my chest.

At first, I thought that was just part of being a good mom—putting your child first, no matter what. But eventually, I had to ask: how could it possibly be good for my son if I was shrinking myself in the process?

That was the beginning of a different rhythm. One where my motherhood didn't erase my individuality. One where both could exist—side by side. Because as long as I felt like I had to choose, I was always going to choose being a mom first. And I don't regret that. But I do know now: it should've never felt like a choice.

There was a time I was so obsessed with giving my child a "healthy" two-parent household that I almost convinced myself to buy a house and get married when my soul was screaming for something else. I had this internal checklist: family, house, career—do it all, and do it quickly, because you already had a child "out of order." But it didn't feel right. And when I finally let myself ask if I even wanted those things, the answer was no. I wanted peace. Support. Freedom. Not a mortgage and a marriage I wasn't confident in.

One day—during a really low point in my mental health—I made a quick, almost impulsive decision to leave my parents' house and move into my own space. It was the first time in a long time that my old self showed back up. The one who trusted her gut. Who moved quickly when something felt right. Even though she showed up out of survival, I was so glad she was still in there. I needed more of her.

Some of the hardest thoughts to process during that time were the ones that sounded positive on the surface. "You're finally taking your mental health seriously—for your family." "You're becoming better for your child." That sounded like growth. But I didn't realize what I was losing in the process until it was already gone.

I had started to resent my son's dad. I felt betrayed. Like I had sacrificed my individuality to hold our family together—and we didn't even make it. But that resentment faded when I took accountability: no one asked me to do that. No one told me to lose myself. I did that. I was trying to live out an image of what a "good mom" or a "real woman" looked like. I bought into a story I didn't actually write.

And it wasn't just about dreams—I let go of little things too. Like rest. Joy. Play. Doing nothing just because I wanted to. If I wasn't fixing something, healing something, or working on being the best mom and partner, I wasn't relaxing—I was depressed. There was no in-between. No neutral. Just pressure.

And a lot of that pressure came from me. Some came from the people around me. And some came from what I imagined people were thinking. But I internalized it all. The message was: you did this out of order, so now you have to ace everything else.

That's exactly what I tried to do. I poured everything into "being better"—into fixing myself, fixing my relationship, and performing like I had it all together. But I made my life a project. I treated my healing like it had a deadline. And in the process, I put pressure on my partner too—pressure he didn't deserve.

I don't regret wanting to be better. But I regret how it made me feel. Like I was never enough. And I regret how I projected that energy onto someone else.

So much of that season felt lonely. Not because people weren't there—but because I didn't even know how to explain what I was going through. I barely had the words for it myself. And no one ever asked.

There wasn't one big moment when I felt like I had to choose between being me and being a mother. It was a slow fade. A series of silent trades. Until one day I looked around and realized: I didn't know who I was without the title.

What brought me back to myself—just a little—was when I hit a breaking point. My relationship was unraveling. My mental health was at an all-time low. And I knew I needed space. A change of environment.

This time, I didn't run. I didn't take a vacation to escape my reality—I created one to face it. I called it a hiatus. Somewhere warm.

Somewhere still. I took my son with me and stayed for several weeks. I didn't just rest—I reflected. I went to therapy. I journaled. I prayed. I sat in it. And I didn't let what anyone might think stop me, because I knew deep in my soul: this wasn't just for Joi the mom. This was for Joi the woman. Period.

That was always the tension. The space between who I was and who I was becoming. Between the life I thought I needed, and the one I was slowly realizing I wanted.

And that's where the gray lived too.

The Understanding

The moment I realized I was deeply unhappy—when I looked at my life and couldn't find joy in the day-to-day, when I noticed how little my child saw me genuinely smile—that was the moment everything shifted.

An unhappy mother couldn't possibly be what was best for my child. That's when I gave myself permission to rewrite what being a good mom looked like. I used to believe it meant always putting him first. But now I understand—putting myself first isn't a threat to his well-being. It's the key to it.

Because the version of me that prioritizes her mental health, her joy, her peace, and her purpose? That version is a better mother. Not because she loves her child more—but because she made space to love herself, too. And from that space, the love multiplies.

When I moved to Atlanta and created a space that finally felt like mine, something shifted. I found myself more present with my son. And yes—I had a moment of guilt. I wondered if maybe I hadn't loved him enough before. But it wasn't about more or less. It was about being more full, more whole. There was simply more of me to give.

One moment I'll never forget happened three weeks after I moved. I was at my first networking event in Atlanta—an award ceremony for screenwriters and filmmakers—when I ended up talking with a producer. I opened up about how I'd always dreamed of living abroad, and how I wasn't sure that dream was "allowed" now that I was a mom. His response? "Can you imagine what that kind of experience could open up for your child?"

That changed everything. It reminded me that maybe the dream isn't just for me. Maybe it's legacy. Maybe by chasing what feels authentic and expansive, I'm giving my son permission to live expansively too. That conversation helped me stop viewing my dreams as selfish and start seeing them as a gift.

I also had to release the guilt I used to carry around not considering my son in every single thing. Of course I consider him. But I no longer believe that everything I enjoy must serve him directly. Some things are just for me. And that's okay. If it doesn't harm him, it doesn't have to benefit him either.

When it comes to balance, I no longer think of it as a 50/50 split. I define balance as a rhythm. A rhythm that works for every version of me. For the mother. The dreamer. The overthinker. The woman of God. The creative. The adventurer. The parts that are loud. The parts that are still healing. Not every part gets equal time—but every part gets a voice. And that's enough.

And the tug-of-war? Between stability and freedom? It's still here. But I'm learning that compromise doesn't have to mean sacrifice. That I don't have to give up the most vibrant parts of me to be a good mom. That I can be both rooted and free.

If my child ever reads this... if he ever truly sees all of me—past, present, and becoming—I hope he learns that selflessness doesn't mean self-abandonment. That choosing yourself can be the most loving thing you do for the people who depend on you. That being responsible doesn't mean you have to stop being who you are. And that the best version of you will always be the one that feels whole—not the one that splits themselves in two.

So whether you're a parent, or simply someone carrying a responsibility that's overtaken your identity—this is for you. This chapter is about not shrinking to fit the roles the world has handed you. It's about giving yourself permission to expand. Because that's where your full self lives. It was never God's intention—to have you live small. And it shouldn't be yours either. Let the version of you who's always been there walk beside the one you're becoming. Let them guide you home.

That, to me, is balance.

Chapter 12: The Gray Area of Capacity

The Power of Showing Up Fully

The Unpacking

One day I was scrolling on Instagram, and this woman I follow—she's a successful entrepreneur —posted a video of herself walking into her business. She said the reason her business is thriving is simple: she gives it 100%, no matter what. That stuck with me.

I found myself sitting there, phone in hand, asking: What have I ever given 100% of myself to? Not just showed up for. Not just finished. But truly poured myself into—fully, consistently, and completely. When I say 100%, I don't mean perfect. I mean showing up with whatever my full capacity is that day—and offering that.

At first, it triggered a little shame. A little regret. A little comparison. She's older than me, but I couldn't help wondering—where would my businesses be, where would I be, if I had given more? I started reflecting hard. I sat with the question: What have I actually given my all to—consistently?

I thought about my college degree. Yes, I finished. Yes, I went to a prestigious school. But my grades could've been better. I didn't apply myself as hard as I could have because I didn't have to. And that pattern didn't stop there. I saw it in other areas of my life too—where "good enough" replaced "my best."

I thought about motherhood, too. Even in one of the areas where I feel most confident, my mind still went to moments where I knew I could have been more intentional, more present, more patient.

I thought about relationships, and my very first session with my new therapist. He told me I hadn't opened myself up to anyone 100%. Even if I gave someone 80, I always kept that last 20 tucked away. He understood why—but he also challenged me to ask: What if you're not protecting yourself as much as you think? What if you're actually cheating yourself? Those questions hit me harder than I expected.

And the more I reflected, the more I realized something that honestly broke my heart a little. Even the times when I tried to show up more fully—even if it wasn't a perfect 100%—it was almost always tied to someone else.

I didn't originally start therapy for me. I started it to be a better mother to my son. To be a better partner to his dad. And although my healing eventually became about me, it still shook me to realize that at the beginning, I wasn't my own reason.

That realization made me emotional. It made me ask:

Why don't I feel worthy enough to be the reason I give my best? Why does it always have to be tied to someone else's needs or love or expectations before I finally decide to pour into myself?

And then there was another layer I had to confront—the inconsistency. I realized I don't always struggle to give my all—I just struggle to give it consistently.

When I'm screenwriting, for example, and an idea sparks something in me—when I can see the scenes and hear the dialogue in my mind—I'm all gas, no brakes. Especially if there's a deadline. Deadlines have always pushed me in a good way. They pull something focused and fierce out of me. But even when there's no external deadline, if the creativity is flowing naturally, I'm in it. I'm giving everything.

Until I'm not.

Because that's when the little devils creep in: The guilt. The doubt. The uncertainty. The fear.

The questions get loud: Is this even good? Will anyone see what I see? Will anyone feel what I feel? What if this is all for nothing?

And slowly, my energy starts to drain. My momentum starts to disappear.

It even happened with this book. When I first started writing Somewhere in the Gray, I was on fire. I had a goal for when I wanted it finished—and as crazy as it sounded, I was actually on track to meet it. Chapter after chapter poured out of me. The excitement was real.

But the closer it got to the part where I'd have to actually release it into the world—the part where people would have access to the parts of me I had only just started embracing—that's when the insecurity crept in. That's when the fear of being misunderstood, overlooked, or exposed got louder. The same thing that once fueled me—the idea of people reading it—started intimidating me. And before I knew it, days were passing without me touching the book at all.

It wasn't a lack of talent. It wasn't a lack of passion. It was a slow, silent surrender to fear.

And the reality is... even though the capacity to show up fully still exists, that is where most of my effort leaks out. Not at the start. Not in the moments of fire and vision. But somewhere in the in-between. Where doubt lives. Where results aren't guaranteed. Where showing up still feels risky.

The Understanding

Sitting with these truths didn't break me. It freed me. Because when I started talking about it with the people around me—asking them, what have you given 100% of yourself to?—I realized I wasn't alone. One of my friends said something that stuck with me: she'd given 100% in moments, but not consistently across the full journey. And like I stated before, I could relate to this. I've touched 100% before. I know what it feels like to be fully locked in.

And when I thought about those moments—when I truly gave my all—I realized they weren't just about outcomes. They were about who I became while doing it.

One of the clearest examples is how I advocate for my son. There have been times where doctors weren't giving 100%, and I absolutely refused to let that be the reason my child suffered.

I remember one moment in 2024, right after my 27th birthday. While I was away celebrating, my son got sick again—a recurrence of issues tied to his condition. When I got back home, I told myself: The next time we go to the hospital, I'm not leaving until they actually solve this. I demanded they take the more extensive steps they had only casually mentioned before. And they finally did. It was difficult—but it was what he needed. And he's been fine ever since.

Those moments—those bold, all-in moments—aren't filled with regret. They're filled with pride. Because when you give your full capacity, even if the experience is hard, you know you honored yourself—and the people you love—completely. And it's those memories that shifted my mindset.

I stopped asking, why I haven't consistently given 100% before. I started imagining what could happen if I choose to now. Consistency isn't built on constant motivation. It's built on self-discipline. It's built on catching the moments when fear tries to creep in—and choosing to block it out, or even allowing it in and still doing the thing anyway. Remind yourself why you started, and speak life into your own process.

Because if I only push forward when the outcome looks guaranteed, I'm not really betting on myself. I'm betting on comfort. And comfort has never been where my growth lived. Giving 100% doesn't guarantee easy outcomes. But it does guarantee alignment—with the person I'm called to be.

Now, I understand that self-discipline isn't punishment. It's self-love in motion. It's standing by yourself even when results aren't instant. It's committing to seeing what happens when you don't quit at the first sign of fear. That's where I am now. Taking inventory. Rooting for myself. Protecting my momentum by protecting my mind. Telling myself: You are worthy of the life you are capable of creating. You are worthy of seeing your full capacity reflected back at you in the life you build.

When guilt, fear, or uncertainty start whispering, "What if this doesn't work?" That's when momentum dies. That's when it starts to feel like—'Well, what's the point?" And that's when I have to remember: The point is me. The point is believing that the life I want—the dreams I have—the stories I'm called to tell—are worth fighting for. Even when it's quiet. Even when results don't come immediately. Even when fear tries to make me sit still.

Now, I'm learning to protect my momentum the same way I protect my peace. To guard it from discouragement. To nurture it when motivation fades. To keep choosing consistency over comfort. To root for myself when doubt creeps in. To remember that my job isn't controlling the outcome—it's showing up with my full self every day I'm able.

God has given me gifts, resilience, tools, and vision. I refuse to waste them anymore. I'm ready to show up fully with others—but even more so for myself. Because I'm worthy of my own best. I'm worthy of seeing what my full effort can produce.

That's what the gray has taught me. This isn't about shame. It's not about hustle. It's not even about perfection. It's about choice. Choosing to show up. Choosing to believe. Choosing to try—again and again—even when the outcome is still uncertain.

The gray area of capacity is where self-honesty meets self-grace. Where potential and patience have to learn how to live together. Where you stop waiting on certainty—and start betting on yourself anyway. And now? Now, I'm betting on myself.

A Letter to the Other Side

For the Black-and-White Thinkers

First and foremost, thank you.

Thank you for making it this far—for reading this book, even though it may not reflect your usual way of thinking. Thank you for giving my perspective a chance, even if it challenged the clarity and certainty you typically hold close. That means something to me. And honestly, it means something to the world.

Let me start by saying: I don't believe there's a "right" or "wrong" way to think. I'm not here to convince anyone to abandon what's always worked for them. I believe in the beauty of individuality. What's true for one person may not land the same for someone else. And that's okay. There's room for all of us.

But what I do believe—what I hope this book has gently revealed—is that there is growth, strength, and deep, meaningful insight in simply considering another perspective. Not because you have to agree with it. Not because it has to replace what you already believe. But because it might offer something. A layer. A nuance. A pause.

Whether it affirms your beliefs, challenges them, or simply lives alongside them, considering the gray offers something valuable.

I also want to take a moment to acknowledge what's powerful about the way you think. Many people who lean toward black-and-white thinking are decisive. They know what they believe, and they stand on it. And that kind of clarity is a strength. Knowing what you want—and being bold enough to act on it—is powerful. I admire that.

My hope is that, through these pages, you've gotten a taste of the good that can come from exploring the gray, too. The peace that can come from withholding judgment until you've sat with the full story. The freedom that comes with not rushing to name something as "right" or "wrong," but instead taking the time to ask why.

Because sometimes, things really are more complex than they look on the surface. Sometimes, important details are left out of the conversation. And when we move too quickly—when we jump to extremes without context—it can lead to impulsive decisions. Misunderstandings. Lasting consequences.

So thank you.

Thank you for not being closed-minded.

Thank you for being willing to sit with discomfort. Thank you for sharing space with, and making space for, those of us whose minds don't land easily on one side or the other.

Some of us were born to live in the nuance. We don't do well with clean lines. We overthink. We explore. We ask a lot of questions before we make a call. And while that can feel frustrating to someone who finds comfort in clarity, I hope this book helped you see the why behind it.

Even if the gray never becomes your home, I hope you'll visit more often. You never know what wisdom you'll walk away with.

A Letter to the Like-Minded

To Those Who Lean Into The Gray

Thank you.

Thank you for being in this community of gray with me. Thank you for not leaving me lonely in my way of thinking. Thank you for showing me that there is something sacred, something beautiful, about a mind that overthinks sometimes. A mind that questions. That wants to know why. That doesn't just accept the first answer handed to it. That looks at the world and says, "Wait... but what about—?" even when everyone else seems content to just move along.

Thank you for being the one who raises an eyebrow when others are silent. The one who challenges the answers, challenges the status quo, and more importantly—challenges your own way of thinking as you grow. Thank you for keeping your heart open while you do it. For keeping your mind open to different views, different angles, different truths.

I see you. I am you. I'm with you in this.

There is nothing wrong with the way your mind works. You're not complicated. You're not being "too deep" or "too much" or "too difficult." You're considerate. You're detailed. You're thoughtful. You want to see the full picture—which is fair. That's wise. You are mindful. You are inquisitive. You are curious. And those things aren't flaws. They are gifts.

So please—don't let anyone's confusion about how you process the world convince you that there's something wrong with you.

And yes, I know sometimes this way of thinking can feel heavy. Sometimes it slows you down. Sometimes it makes decisions harder. Sometimes it causes you to loop things over in your mind for days when everyone else has already moved on. But that doesn't mean you need to change who you are. Just shift how you use it. Make it work for you. Channel your depth into something meaningful. Don't abandon your process—refine it so that it's still productive. Still powerful. Still pushing your life forward.

And as you do all that? Stay rooted in self-love. Stay anchored in self-respect. So that your deep capacity for understanding never becomes something others take advantage of. So that your grace doesn't become someone else's excuse.

I'll also say this—don't be afraid of black-and-white thinking. It has its place. It can serve you, too. Don't be afraid to land on a decision. To draw a line. To say yes or no without over-explaining. Just don't abandon the part of you that loves to sit in the gray and see the full picture first. Because that part of you? That's your power.

It's okay if your process is long. It's okay if it's layered. It's okay if it doesn't fit into a quote or a quick caption. If you're too much for the room you're in, then it's not the room for you.

So be confident in who you are. Stand beside the black-and-white thinkers—but don't shrink next to them. And don't assume either of you is better than the other. Just different. Just beautifully wired in your own way.

And if—for any reason—this book moved you closer to one side, even if it pulled you away from the gray... I still thank you for being here. For having ever been here. For journeying through these pages with me. For letting yourself see what this lens had to offer.

Whatever you took away from this book, I just hope you feel seen. I hope you feel heard. I hope you feel understood. I hope you know there's space in the world for you—and that your complex, beautiful, thoughtful mind is a gift.

You're a gift.

We're a gift.

I love you.

About the Author

Joi Renee is an author and screenwriter—but more personally, she's a mother to a vibrant little boy named Casyn. She's a daughter, a sister, a niece, a friend, and a safe space for those who know her—and even those who don't. Whether in real life or through her words, Joi shows up as a confidant, a witness, and someone who holds space for truth without judgment.

Her heart is rooted in storytelling, healing, and helping people feel seen through the kind of words that linger long after the page is turned. Like many, she's found herself in a career that doesn't fully reflect her passion or purpose—but it's helped keep the lights on and the snacks stocked. Now, she's stepping more boldly into the calling she's always known was hers: writing stories that live in the gray, where truth and nuance meet.

Somewhere in the Gray is her debut book—but it's far from the last.

If you've made it to this page, know this—she considers you a new friend now.

You can connect with Joi on Instagram at @JoiReneeTheWriter.

Thank you for sitting with me.

— Joi Renee

www.ingramcontent.com/pod-product-compliance
Lightning Source LLC
Chambersburg PA
CBHW020418150626
46554CB00014B/1939